GET VIRAL

VIDEO MARKETING
Everything You Wanted To know But Didn't Know To Ask

Copyright © 2015 F.R. Awde Consulting

Get Viral
Version 1, February 2016
F. R. Awde Consulting
rome@romeawde.com
Beaumont, Alberta Canada
587-434-1938

Table of Contents

GET VIRAL

VIDEO MARKETING
Everything You Wanted To
know But Didn't Know To Ask

Rome Awde

http://romeawde.com

Introduction

Get Viral with Video Marketing. Simply put, this is one of the most engaging, influential and potentially profitable forms of marketing.

Video has the ability to grab attention and to help you establish authority in ways that no other form of marketing can approach. So it's absolutely vital that you start leveraging this type of marketing in your business as soon as possible.

In fact, video marketing is so powerful that it could very well be all that you need in order to get the word out about your business.

If you are already using video marketing, then it is just as important to ensure that you are doing so effectively.

Video marketing, when done well, is incredibly powerful but if your videos don't have the professional quality that your viewers expect, then they could actually do harm to your business and reputation.

It is essential that you are not just incorporating video into your marketing but that you are also doing so in the best way possible.

By picking up this book, you have taken the first step towards growing your business and throughout the following chapters, we will be looking in depth at how to create and share fantastic, high-quality videos that will accelerate sales and put your business into a position that you have dreamed about.

What you are going to learn from this book:

You will learn what video marketing is, how marketing videos are generally used and what different kinds of videos there are for marketing purposes.

I'll show you why video marketing is such an amazing shortcut to take your business to any level you desire, thanks to the extremely targeted traffic you can get. You will see the benefits videos can bring to your business and online marketing efforts.

I will show you 14 amazing facts that will open your eyes to the immense power of videos for marketing in today's business environment.

You will see how businesses are using videos in their marketing efforts, so you can have complete confidence in this powerful marketing strategy for your own business.

You will learn about the top video sharing sites, their benefits, as well as how each of them can help you get the most out of video marketing.

You will learn about some excellent video marketing tools, highly effective tools that have been created to make videos amazingly simple for you, even if you haven't created a single video in your life.

You'll also learn how to do video marketing the right way from start to finish using one of the most effective and easy to apply video marketing methods.

We'll cover topics like creating, uploading, optimizing and promoting your video.

We'll also cover several highly effective video marketing tricks you can apply and see some great results in your efforts. Proven tricks as used by experienced business owners.

Learn about the hottest ways to use video for marketing, so you don't have to be on your own out there trying to figure out what's actually working.

We'll take an in depth look at a few video marketing case studies. These are actual examples to show you how video marketing actually works and its effectiveness.

I will give you a list of all video 'Dos' you must include in your video marketing and a list of all 'Don'ts' that you'll want to avoid in your campaigns.

Finally, we will cover all of the "Tech" in creating your first marketing video. I will cover cameras, lighting, backgrounds, script writing and how you can do it all for little to no money.

Well let's dig into video marketing for your business. Enjoy the read and use these valuable strategies in your offline or online business marketing to Get Viral.

In Success,

Rome Awde
romeawde.com

Chapter 1
What is Video Marketing

Video marketing is marketing via the medium of video on the web. In many cases, this means creating videos and uploading them to YouTube, though that is only one option.

Video marketing is a growing and ideal way to promote products and services to increase traffic on your website or through the front door. This type of marketing has become very popular and highly effective when done correctly.

Videos have been used by Internet Marketers to sell their products and services using a form of video called a "Sales Video". Internet marketers almost always include usable data in a video for user engagement to optimize the sales message.

Videos are generally used by businesses to build brand awareness of their company and products. These videos have been mostly about information to increase customer interest in the brand with less focus on selling the actual product. My goal is to help change that trend. Small business can also effectively use video to sell directly.

People will purchase products when they watch an online video of that product instead of reading the reviews and specifications, which means you can utilize the power of video to convert more sales.

Types of Videos for Marketing Purposes

Video is a highly captivating medium. Videos are inherently used to keep a potential customer engaged, generate awareness and create a mental picture of a product or service.

As a result, video has become a standard medium for communication and marketing activities.

Image manipulation has been made simpler, and so demonstrating the use of products has also been made much easier.

Remember that seeing is more engaging than hearing, and seeing and hearing is even more effective.

Below are some of the types of videos for marketing purposes.

Animated video: You can use video creation sites like GoAnimate.com and XtraNormal.com to create motion graphic videos. On the other hand, if you want to have high-end motion graphics you can use Adobe AfterEffects.

Video E-mail: This is a great new way to engage and connect with your prospective customer and colleagues. You can simply record a video through your webcam and free websites which include MailVu.com and Eyejot.com. This makes your business stand out and passes a visual message to the customer instead of using traditional written emails.

Customer testimonial video: Testimonials enable customers to tell stories in their own voice. They give their experience on the usage of a product or service. This creates a powerful resource for marketing. You can use the Brainshark tool to put the presentation together. You can use them in your sales videos or on a web site.

Webinar Video: You can also create webinar videos. You record it using GoToWebinar.com or Instant Teleseminar. These videos illustrate the products and services you sell. You can post them on your web site or YouTube.

Launch series: These are released as a series of videos. They are content heavy and should grab the attention of prospective customers. Their main aim is to establish credibility before releasing the final sales video.

Video PowerPoint: This is a commonly used video presentation tool especially for seminars. It is powerful because it allows the use of music and narration. You can use this as a marketing tool during product promotion.

Interview videos: Use Skype or the free Google hangouts to create interview videos. The interview can focus on two people – that is, the interviewee and the interviewer – or can be a 'news style' format. News style is where you are the interviewee on a subject on camera with an interviewer off camera.

First impression video: This video gives a direct appeal about a product. You can use it as the first video on your homepage. It is used for personal and promotional videos. You can also use it as a general advertisement for your business.

Video Tips series: This is still one of the most popular uses of video. It is ideal for improving your search optimization and establishing your presence on YouTube. They are a huge help in building credibility and showing you as an expert in your specialization or niche.

Chapter 2
Why Video Marketing?

Benefits for Offline and Online Business

Easy Access: People are now able to access videos with their mobile devices and smartphones. The customer can see your videos from anywhere in the world. Because of this level of availability, you are able to reach a large number of potential customers, especially if you're an international company.

Informative: Most people are interested in video in order to get information quickly. If you create an information video, it will give you more targeted results. If you present your products and services on video in an effective way, people will want to see more from you.

Multifaceted: Use video to promote your brand, product, services, educating or training your clients and more. You can use your video on social media like Facebook and Twitter. However, be sure that your website is linked to your social media sites.

Reputation: People prefer to do business with those they trust. Video helps prospective customers get to know you more easily than ordinary written words can. The goal is they'll hopefully learn to like and trust you, and become a long term customer.

Low cost: Video marketing is cheaper than other methods of advertising. When you compare the cost of video with the value you get from it, you will find the expense is minimal and the results can be excellent. Create it once then it can be viewed as many times as your audience wants.

Demonstrations: Product demonstration with video is an effective way to introduce your product or service to your audience. Reviews, case studies, product promotion videos and examples should be included in video to increase sales.

Influence: The classic horror movie is a great example of how audio has an emotional effect on us. The creepy music comes in, immediately cluing you in that something bad is about to happen. Imagine combining that audio with powerful video to influence the emotions of the viewer and create a much more compelling message than with just written words alone.

Stand out: Video marketing is easier and more affordable than ever, so including a marketing video on your website increases awareness about your brand to stand your company and products or services apart from the competition. A video enables you to gain an extra edge over other businesses.

Go viral: Today everyone wants to go viral. Audiences are always looking for the next viral sensation. For your message you can create an awesome and exciting video explaining to them the uniqueness, benefits, and core values about your business, product and services. Think Winnebago Man as been a negative promotional video that maintained the Winnebago brand for a generation.

Relationships: With all businesses, personal connection with your clients is the biggest selling factor in your market. When you are creating a video for your potential buyers, you have to remind them that you care for them. Nurturing your client by building and maintaining relationships takes time but a video can do it in less time.

Wow factor: Video adds a punch to your marketing that text marketing can't. If videos are impressive and effective, they provoke viewers in such way that is not possible with the written word. When viewers find your video interesting or useful, they show your video to others. This shows their interest in your product and services.

Traffic: People are watching 6 billion hours of video on YouTube monthly. Google, whom owns YouTube, gives high priority in search ranking if you have YouTube videos. Video marketing provides the best opportunity to reach millions of potential customers.

Soft selling: You can create informative videos of your product and service. When you upload a video online, it decreases your effort and increases your success rate. While viewers play your video, it can include soft sales messages, as well as information and web links to your business.

Eye Opening Video Facts

YouTube attracts 136MM unique viewers per month. (source: NIELSEN)	Two-thirds of the world's mobile data traffic will be video by 2016. (source: Cisco)
36% of online consumers trust video ads. (source: Nielsen Wire)	87% of online marketers use video content. (source: Outbrain)
76% of marketers plan to increase their use of YouTube and video marketing. (source: Social Media Examiner)	49% of the top 20% of B2B marketers in generating leads through social media integrate online video with social media, compared to the industry average of 32%. (source: Aberdeen)
Video ads make up 35% of total online ad spending, up from 27% in 2011. (source: Break Media)	Digital video advertising spend will reach $5.4B by 2016. (source: Break Media)
49% of U.S. marketers plan to boost video ad spending in 2012, and 65% have larger mobile ad budgets. (source: eMarketer)	Rich media ads with video generate 6 times as many post-ad site visits as standard banner ads. (source: MediaMind)
Online video advertisers prefer pre-roll ads by a 3:1 margin over the next most favored format. (source: Break Media)	30 second in-stream mobile video ads have an 88.3% completion rate. (source: Rhythm Insights)

Combining video with full page ads boosts engagement by 22%. (source: Rhythm Insights)	22% of U.S. small businesses plan to post a video to YouTube in the next 12 months to promote their businesses. (source: BIA/Kelsey)

Chapter 3

Are Businesses Doing Video Marketing?

Yes, businesses are using Videos to market their products and services. Here are examples of businesses that use video marketing to inform their audience about their brand.

RevZilla: Founded in 2007, <u>RevZilla</u> Motorsports is a premium in-store and online shopping experience for motorcycle lovers who are looking for helmets, gear, motorcycle jackets and other accessories.

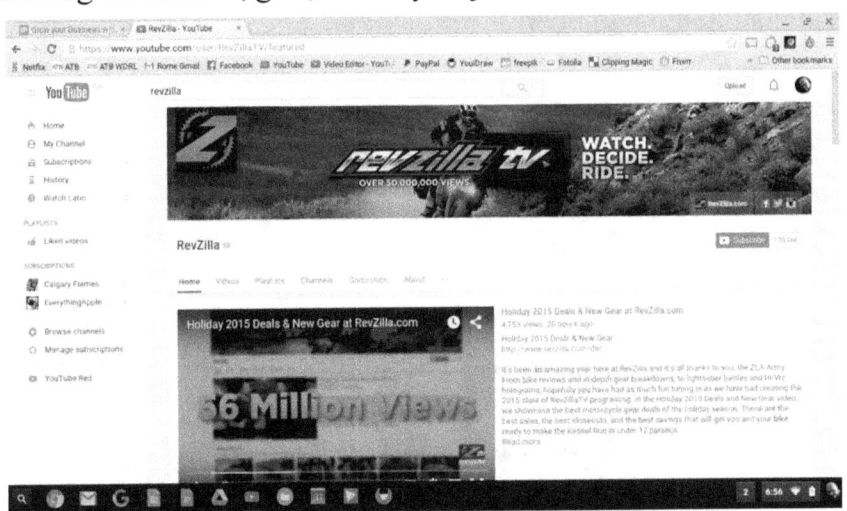

Anthony Bucci says "YouTube connects us with our customers. We use our own voice—not a corporate one—and our customers love us for that."

They use product guide videos, safety tips videos and knowledge driven videos of the services they provide. Their videos have consistently increased their subscriptions, customer loyalty and repeat customers.

They launched a dedicated video channel with TrueView ad campaign to guide their new and old customers to their videos. The videos increased traffic and landed them on their e-commerce website. Also, they focused on customer loyalty.

With over 4500 videos, 170,000 subscribers and 56 million views on their branded YouTube channel, RevZilla achieved 50% growth in their revenue with video marketing. This company's video marketing program is inspiring.

Rokenbok: Rokenbok is a high end robotic toys and construction Systems Company. When the economy took a turn, the company needed newer, less expensive ways to reach their customers and demonstrate how to operate a Rokenbok toy.

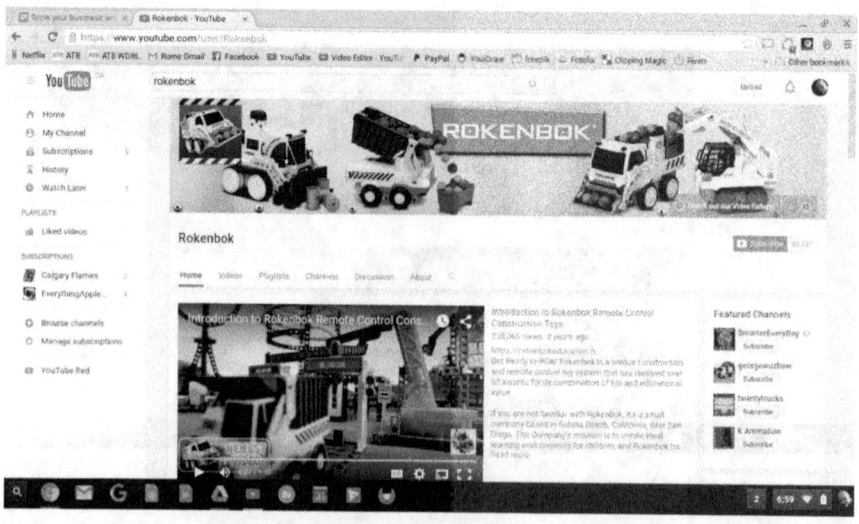

Eichen says, "YouTube is becoming our most important vehicle for advertising. We have transformed ourselves into a classic toy store with only sales online."

Rokenbok started uploading on YouTube using TrueView in search engine and display ads. The aim of the company was to find new ways to demonstrate their toys, build relationships with customers and drive sales with their online e-commerce site.

Building a YouTube channel with videos based on fun and education to target families, they targeted viewers who searched for construction and train related videos. They also maintained a focus on consistent messages to build a relationship with the customers and viewers.

Many of their YouTube Videos have over a million views. Their results have been excellent. YouTube became the number one source of traffic for Rokenbok as upwards of 50% of customers came from YouTube.

American Airlines: American Airlines recently launched a documentary style video series on YouTube named "Behind the Scene" to answer the questions of its customers like "Where does a bag go after it's checked?", "What's involved in taking delivery of a new plane?" and "Why do airfares change so much?" etc.

The creative manager of Social Marketing, Jon Bird said that "Airlines are massive organizations but American Airlines is the world's largest airline organization. There are some messages that are tough to convey, but the ability to create videos can help to make them easily understood".

These videos are not the traditional advertisement that is used for visitors booking a flight with American Airlines.

The goal of these videos is not lead generation; these videos are built to increase brand awareness of American Airlines as a responsive and transparent brand. As of summer 2015, the American Airlines video, 'Behind the Scenes - Creating American Airlines New Look, Logo and Livery' has been viewed 335,000 times. The Company has a subscribers list of 34,000 people.

The Home Depot: Home Depot stands out in their niche market because they publish relevant content for their brand. They know that free educational video content established Home Depot as a trusted brand.

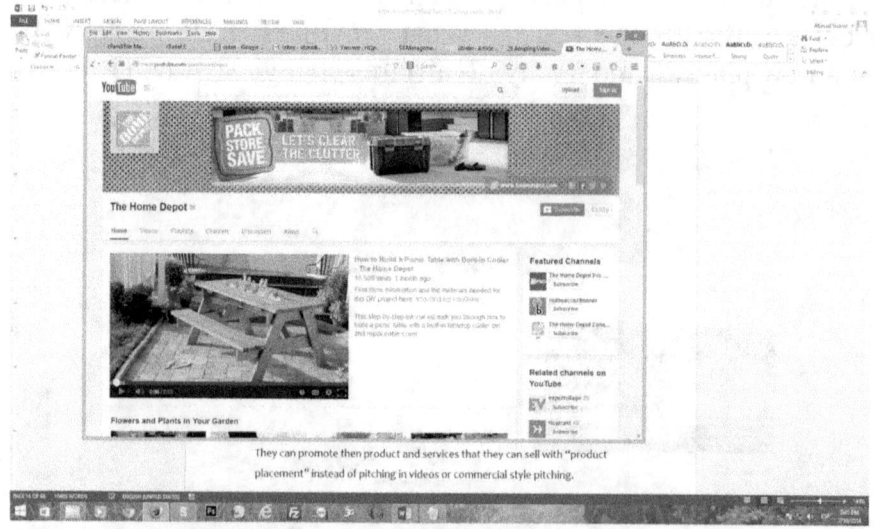

They can promote their products and services and sell them with "product placement" instead of pitching them in videos or commercial style pitching.

Home Depot humanizes its faceless corporation, including their employees in their advertisement campaigns.

Home Depot makes its tutorials simple with straight talking and employees who wear an orange apron and work in their stores to make it more personal.

With over 100,000 subscribers and millions of views on their YouTube channel, The Home Depot has used Video Marketing very effectively.

Ibis: When Accor, Europe's largest hotel operator decided to launch its IBIS brand again, it turned to YouTube videos to get a lift in viewers. More than 100 videos are created by Ibis hotels and many of them have more than a million views.

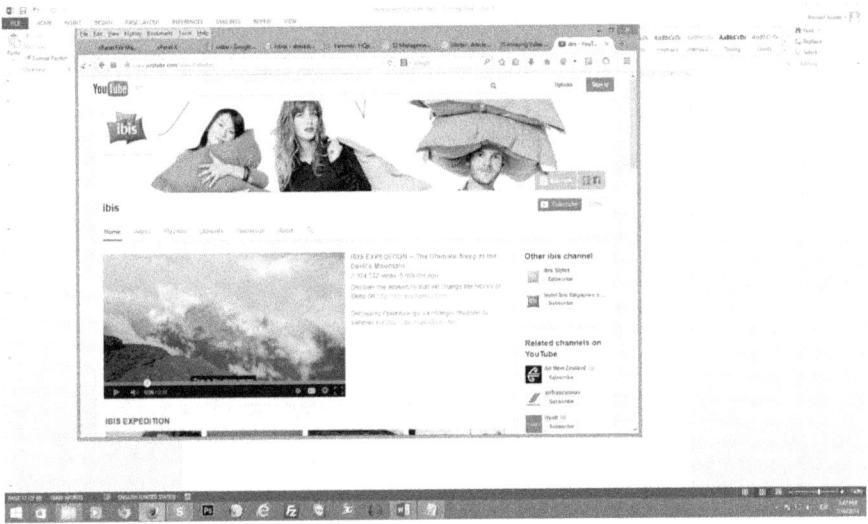

Ibis videos are short and they use old standby videos of cute baby animals to make audiences watch. Ibis uses videos to increase its brand awareness and promote its products and services. Although their YouTube subscribers are relatively low at 5,000, their extremely high viewership makes them a leader in this form of Video Marketing.

Chapter 4
Top Video Sharing Sites

Online video streaming is one of the most, if not 'the' most, popular online pastimes. Video sharing websites have changed the way of looking at media. Video connects viewers who are not connected geographically.

YouTube:

When you think about video sharing websites, YouTube is the first one that comes to mind. It's more popular than TV.

As the stats say, it is the 3rd most visited website in the world and 80% of YouTube traffic comes from outside of the U.S. Over 100 hours of video are uploaded every  minute on YouTube and more than 6 billion hours of video are watched on a monthly basis.

YouTube's paid advertisements and more than 1 billion users make it a clear winner. Google gives priority to YouTube videos in search engine results as it is the parent company of YouTube.

The best part of YouTube is that it provides the ability to watch without becoming a member. You will be able to find videos according to your interest or hobby and if you are a community member you can interact, comment and post videos on those videos.

YouTube video sharing is the best way to collect and display user comments. YouTube provides all the facilities to determine what your potential customer wants to know from you, by letting them post comments on your videos.

A search function makes it easy to search the videos you are looking for - otherwise you can try an advanced search to narrow your search results. Ratings and screenshots make it easier to find the particular video you want to watch or download. YouTube is also the second largest search engine on the Internet after Google.

YouTube also provides access to its customizable features like screen size, volume, watch later, speed, annotation and subscribe options. You can also create a customized playlist of videos. YouTube allows you to embed its videos on other websites, and other websites can simply import videos from YouTube.

You can create and upload videos in your own way. You can identify your audience as they comment or post replies on video. You can also restrict the audience for your video. When uploading a video, you can specify the place where it was shot; you can upload it with your cell phone.

Before posting a video, you need a title, short description, category and a set of tags to help with search on YouTube.

YouTube also provides a special upload manager that decreases the uploading time and increases the streaming process.

YouTube video content should be less than 2 GB and shorter than 15 minutes. Advanced options are also available.

YouTube supports AVI, MOV, WMV and MPG formats. When you upload videos on YouTube, YouTube converts video files to adobe flash formats. Flash format is compatible with most computers.

One thing to remember though is Flash is not supported on iOS devices, such as iPhone or iPad. To watch YouTube video on these devices, you must have the YouTube app for the Apple device.

Vimeo:

Vimeo has more than 100 million unique visitors per month. Vimeo layout is clean and the video player is much bigger than the YouTube player. Content is the star in Vimeo videos. Vimeo also focuses on high definition video quality.

Vimeo is used by professional video makers. It offers a free package, and it also has Plus and Pro paid packages.

The Pro and Plus packages increase your upload limit with more control of your video. Filmmakers often choose Vimeo to promote their films in short clips.

Vimeo allows its basic (or free) members to upload up to 500MB per week and if you want to upload more than 500MB, you can pay Vimeo for Pro and Plus packages.

Video quality of Vimeo is high, so there are tons of high definition videos available on their website. Here you can also create and moderate video groups.

In the Vimeo Plus Package, you will get 5GB per week with extra features like privacy settings, source-file downloading options, unlimited video groups, unlimited video channels and albums.

In the Vimeo Pro package, members are awarded portfolio and review pages. This gives the option to host commercial content. Pro members have unlimited storage space with highly customizable video players, HTML5 support, full mobile, tablet and connected TV compatibility, third party video player support and optional original file storage. Vimeo supports all current video file formats.

Dailymotion:

Dailymotion is the international video sharing site of choice,

with a worldwide audience. It allows users to search, browse and view the videos with keywords, channels and groups.

Dailymotion is available in 34 countries in 16 languages with 100 million audience members.

Dailymotion has an audience-first platform which shows the picture preview of videos and allows them to be shared to Facebook and Twitter. You can share your personal videos with a restricted audience or with the world.

Dailymotion has a flag on each video that points to exactly where the video is generated in the world; this is a unique feature of Dailymotion.

Dailymotion has strict guidelines regarding content. You can upload videos from web cam and mobile.

Two different accounts are offered- Basic and Motionmaker. A Basic account gives you the ability to upload video files up to 60 minutes of length, 4 GB in size and with a HD resolution of 1920 x 1080 pixels.

With the Motionmaker account you will be able to upload videos with no restrictions on size or length, in HD 1920 x 1080 pixels as well as being able to monetize your videos and benefit from exclusive tools and features, including livestreaming capabilities.

Real content by Motionmaker is promoted aggressively on the first page of Dailymotion and in search results. MP4, M4V, WMV, MPEG, MPG, AVI, DIVX, DV, 3GP, FLV, MKV, MOV, and OGG video formats are supported by Dailymotion.

Metacafe:

Metacafe is the oldest video sharing website with 40 million unique visitors per month. Metacafe is focused on commercial videos and specializes in short-form original content videos in the entertainment industry.

Metacafe includes the videos that amaze, inspire and amuse their audience. These videos are initiated and chosen by users with review and reward.

The biggest advantage of Metacafe is having high quality video without multiple copies of the same content, which prevents duplicate videos unlike on YouTube. A video can be uploaded only once.

Metacafe is so popular among people because it is the first video sharing website that pays its audience to upload their videos. After 20,000 views on a video, it pays $5 for every 1000 views on your video, which motivate its members to create great videos with good content to drive traffic for that particular video.

An individual video file must be less than 100 MB, but the length of video is not set. So the quality of a video can be affected by the length of the video.

It's easy finding the videos you are looking for and highly ranked videos are available on the home page. The search function is also easy to use, you can search with criteria and categories or by keywords.

It supports all the current popular video formats.

Vube:

Vube is a new video sharing website launched in January 2013 with 55 million users. But it's growing much faster than other video sharing websites, as it has reached the top 100 most visited websites. Aggressive marketing strategies drive traffic for this website.

If you are an artist and movie maker with a creative mind and

if your videos go viral on the website, you could score in the range of $20 to $10,000. To win a prize, you have to keep your video in the top 25 list for a month to increase your chance to get paid.

You will find the user interface of Vube easy to understand with a proper browsing experience. You can upload your video by following the step by step process of uploading and registering on Vube.

Chapter 5
Video Marketing Power Tools

Video marketing is an awesome way to interact with your audience. You have to tell a story in video to define the benefits of your product and demonstrate the product's effectiveness in order to build your audience's trust in you, which is extremely important to increase your sales and revenue.

Now to make it easier than ever, I am going to show you some really good tools.

Viewbix:

Viewbix is a video marketing tool, which helps you drive more sales and leads. Viewbix also allows you to add interactive apps like contact details, email forms and other apps.

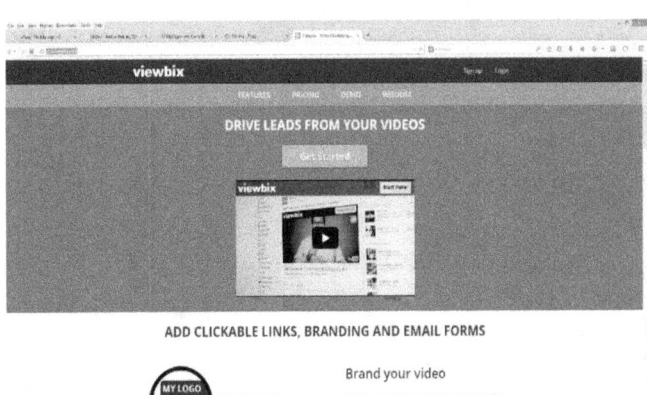

You can brand your video, add email forms to your video and add clickable links in video. You can also add images, music and maps to engage customers. It also provides analytics and reports to measure your conversions, actions and engagement rates.

Tom Telford, owner of Cedar Creek Cabin Rentals said that he was able to add calls to action to their videos with Viewbix and ROI increased by 13%.

GoAnimate:

GoAnimate is an easy tool that allows you to create a professionally animated video. It can be a lot of fun to create videos. First,

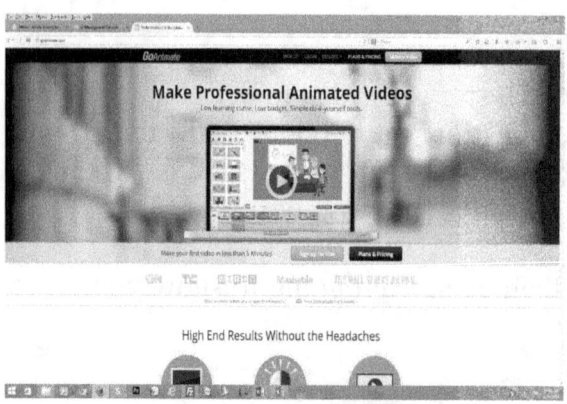

you have to select a theme for your video and which type of video you want to create.

You select a template, different types of characters, shapes, and images to create your video. While creating the video you have options for background and drag and drop sequences. The results will be absolutely amazing.

Camtasia:

Camtasia is the simplest video selling tool with a screen capturing

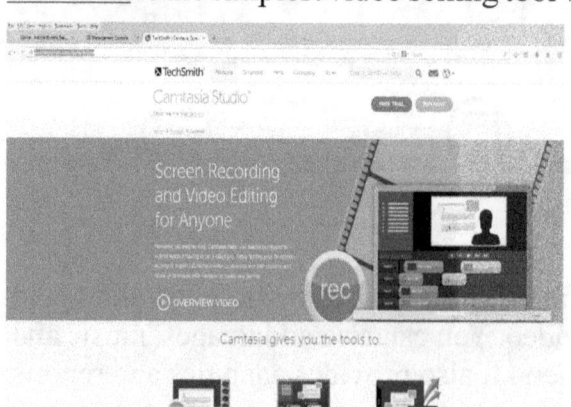

software package. It is effective and will help you demonstrate your product. You can record your screen with its screen-capturing software.

You can create powerful videos

and enhance your videos with Camtasia power editor, themes, animated background, callouts, and graphics.

You can engage your audience and increase your conversions with clickable links, search and more. These videos are easily sharable so viewers can watch anywhere, anytime.

Stupeflix:

Creating videos becomes easier than ever with Stupeflix. You can create a video with music, video and images. It has a basic and pro version.

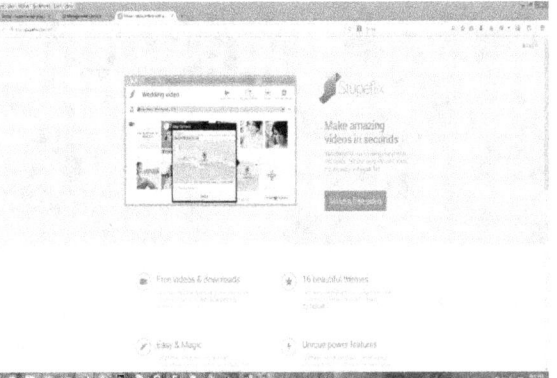

The Basic version is free, and it's available with 16 beautiful themes.

You can add maps, voiceover and trim your videos quickly and easily. You can export them to Facebook, Instagram, Dropbox, and via a URL. It is one click sharable.

EasySketchPro:

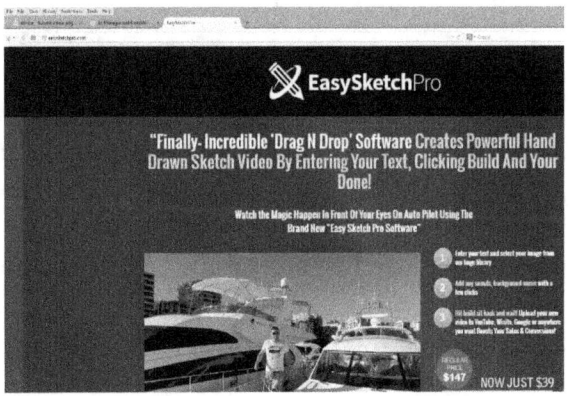

EasySketchPro is a drag and drop software for powerful videos. You just have to enter your text, image with sound, and click the build button and it's done for you.

It is very easy and helpful for businesses and online marketers.

You can create videos for yourself and to promote affiliate programs. You can publish it to YouTube to get good exposure, make them go viral, and build engagement with EasySketchPro videos.

VideoMarkerFX:

VideoMakerFX is a tool that has been adapted by marketers of

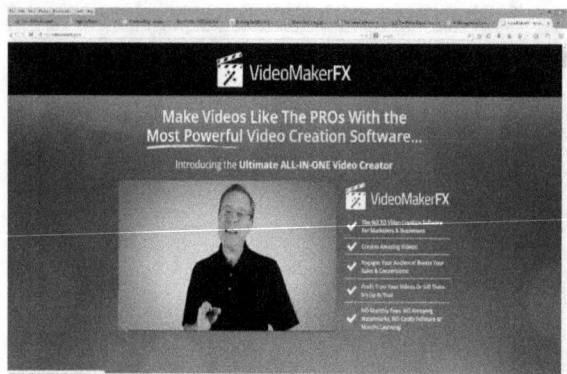

various firms to create great video clips in a few minutes. It's suitable for marketers, because it can create multiple numbers of video clips within a short period of time.

It saves time and makes work easier. It enables many people to create beautiful boards and videos to promote their products and services.

It's the objective of every business to maximize profits by reducing total cost incurred. This is a suitable tool to apply because it's quicker and more efficient in producing video clips.

Powtoon:

This is a marketing tool that contains a combination of presentations from Powerpoint to animated cartoons. Powtoon helps people create animated features such as cartoon features that can be used to present an advertisement.

It's a basic marketing tool that has been used by many businesses to attract customers to their sites.

Animated features influence the products of the company. It creates beautiful video clips with presentations that can be used to advertise products. Marketers have used this tool to create television Ads, video

clips, business portfolios and to draw invitations thus promoting the business.

Magisto:

Magisto is a tool that is used to create movies. It can change your daily photos and recorded video into videos you will always enjoy watching.

It takes your beautiful photos and recorded videos and adds animations, effects, and transitions that best suits your interests.

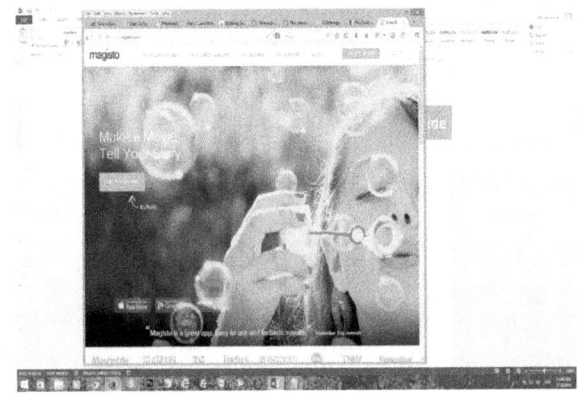

Magisto uses a proprietary Emotion Sense Technology. This allows users to collaborate with artificial intelligence to ensure that their Movie elicits the right sort of emotional response.

Users provide footage and supply emotional direction through choice of music and video style and Magisto brings their footage to life in a Movie that not only compiles the best moments of uploaded footage, but also captures a mood.

Prezi:

If you want to captivate your audience anytime you give a presentation, then this is the best tool to use. It allows you 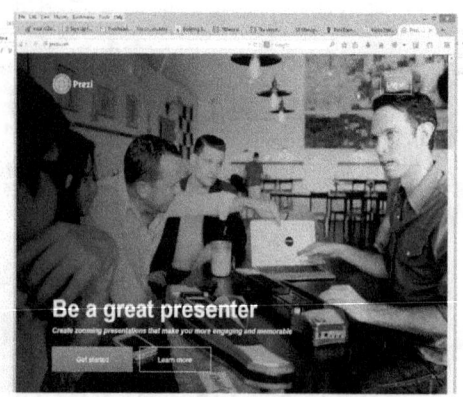 to make your story more interesting by zooming through it. It creates images and animations that make your presentation look more attractive to your audience.

Prezi helps to promote presentations to make them look attractive. It has features that allow the creation of images, decorations, and selection of appropriate themes that best suit your presentation. Many business firms are adopting this method as it creates attractive presentations that appeal to potential customers.

Animoto:

Animoto is a simple tool that allows you to create videos in a 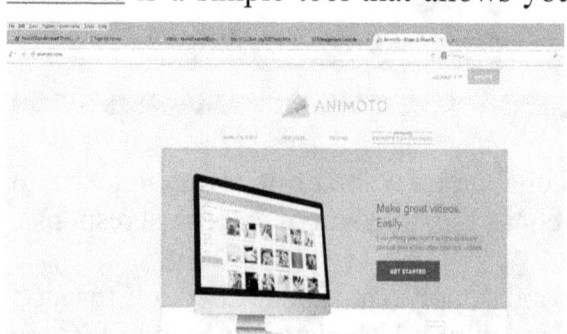 matter of seconds. It allows you to add your favorite photographs, videos and text.

Animoto already has the music that will be added to your

video animations to make it more compelling. Users are able to transfer these video clips to many social media sites such as Facebook, Twitter etc.

Users can choose from a variety of animations to be applied to their video clips. You can pick your favorite music from the library and incorporate it into the video clip.

Chapter 6
How to Do Video Marketing the Right Way

In this step by step process I will show you the easiest, fastest and cheapest way to create a video for business purposes.

The intention of a marketing video is to invite the viewer to visit your website or go directly to your place of business. Videos can have a direct call to action, but primarily they are used to get a prospect to move to a web page that has a call to action.

Marketing video can also be used to demonstrate a product or service, but should still direct a customer to a website.

The video shouldn't be too long. Just attractive enough to make the viewer want to know more, and want to visit your website for further information.

The core steps we will cover in the process are:

Step 1: Create

Step 2: Submit

Step 3: Optimize

Step 4: Advertise

Step 1: Create

In this step we will cover everything you need to know about creating your video from start to finish. We will divide this step into 5 Parts: Deciding on a title, planning, putting together images or video clips, creating/editing the video and downloading your video.

The Title

The first step is to pick the title of your video, and there are several things to be aware of for this extremely important step.

The title should include a keyword inside it, a word or term that is important and if possible, a hot topic in your market. If there is no online audience in your niche, to whom would you be advertising?

You will need to do some research for keywords that may directly identify your business activity. That keyword should represent a real audience online, and that exact audience is who you will be marketing your video to.

It is very important to use the name of your business in the name of your Video, but a popular keyword may be combined with that name at the same time.

People could search for your business name in Google, but you could target a great deal more people by using a hot keyword in the title at the same time.

In this book case we will create a Video for a Cake Decorating small business. What I will do is use a few very good tools and see what the "Cake Decorating" keyword looks like on the web.

There are so many different keyword research tools but I will use the tools provided by websites that are widely used to search for information about any topic online.

The website most used by people to search about any topic online is Google.com.

Google offers excellent keyword research tools to help you identify a hot-buyer audience over the web.

Google offers what is called the Keyword Planner

There are 4 principal components that will tell you if your topic is hot on Google.

✓ **Searches**

The first component of a hot topic is a lot of searches. Here you can see the searches from the Google Keyword Planner. Average monthly search for "cake decorating" is 60,500 in this example.

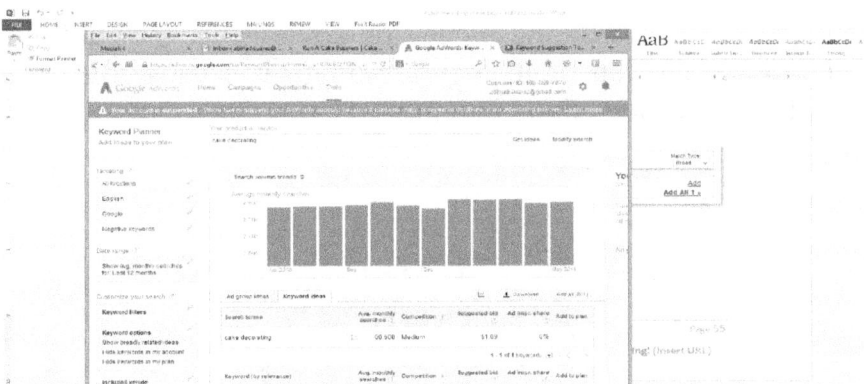

✓ **Advertisers**

The second component of keyword research is the presence of advertisers.

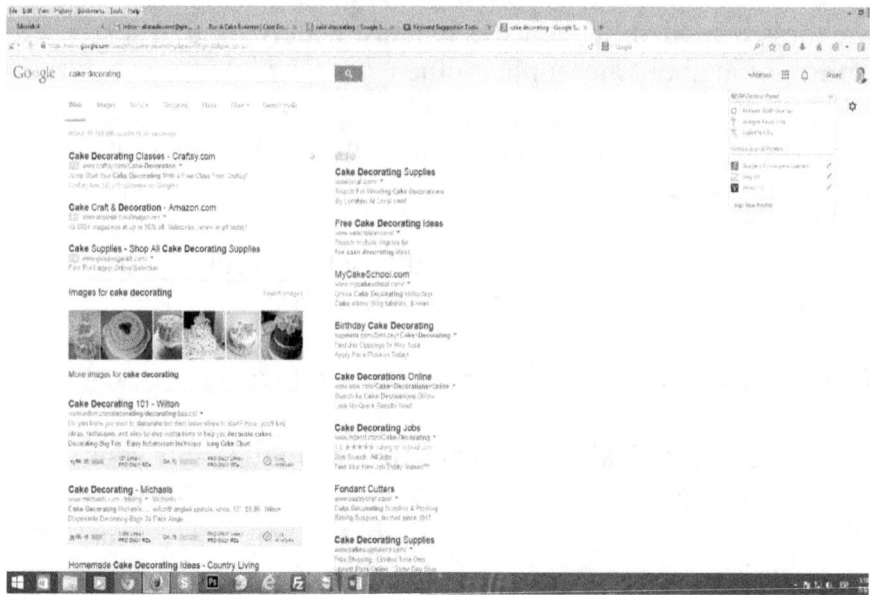

This means marketers are spending money advertising their websites, products and services by using that exact keyword inside their advertising campaigns.

If marketers are spending money on advertising, they are not doing it for the fun of it, they are doing it because they are actually getting something in return.

✓ CPC

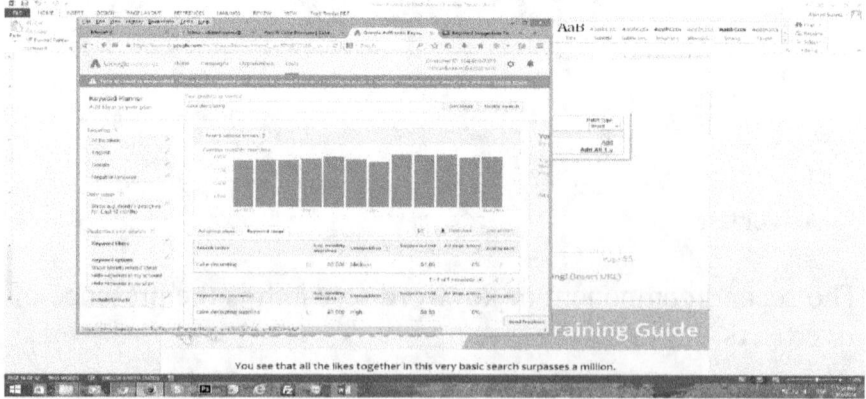

The third component of a hot topic is the 'Cost per Click' value. This is the way you can identify how commercial your topic is. Those advertisers of the second component are spending money for every time someone clicks on their ad. The higher the CPC, the greater the commercial value of that keyword.

If their advertising expenses are high, that means your topic has a committed buyer audience online.

✓ **Affiliate Products**

The fourth Component is one of the most important ones.

It's great to have a very interested audience in your topic, but it's also great to know there are advertisers spending a good amount of money advertising in your topic. But without the existence of products being sold, how can you say your topic is in fact commercial enough for you to market your business online?

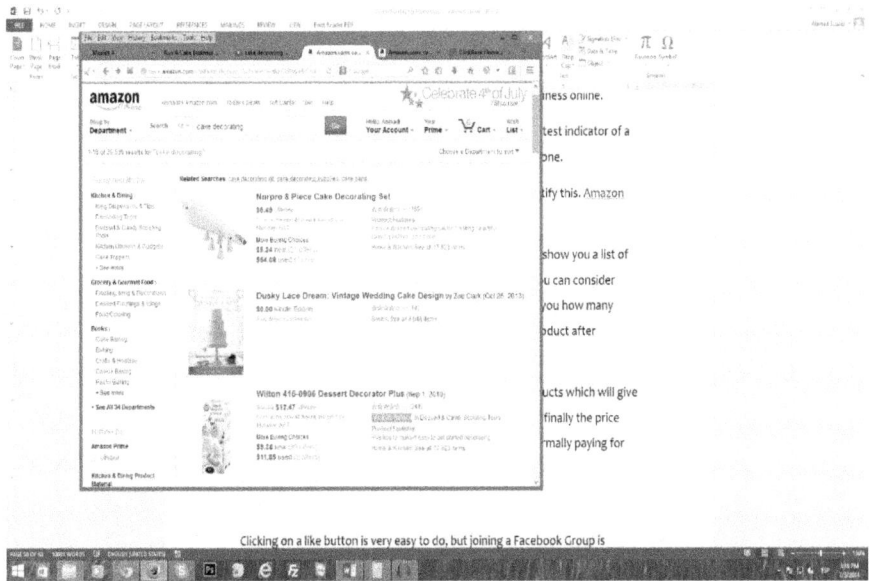

The presence of real products actually being sold is the greatest indicator of a hot selling topic online. No other component can beat this one.

There are two awesome websites where you will be able to identify this. Amazon for Physical Products and ClickBank for Digital Products.

Performing a basic search with your keyword on Amazon will show you a list of products all related to that search.

There are a lot of things you can consider here. You can consider the number of reviews, which will tell you how many buyers have taken the time to leave a testimony about the product after purchasing it and using it.

Another great piece of info you can take from here is the Titles of the products which will give you a very good idea on hot topics to promote in your videos. And finally, the price may tell you what the price point is that this audience is normally paying for products in this topic.

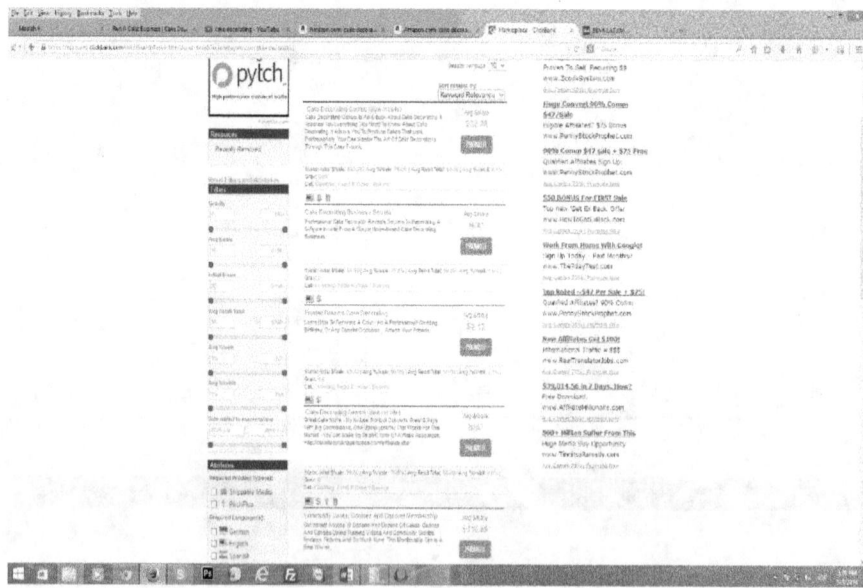

On ClickBank I found a few digital products to promote. It's not that great compared to Amazon, but I can still use those products as examples for topics.

Ok, now that you have found out that your topic is hot and highly profitable on the web, you can create the title of your Video.

My little cake decorating business' name is Cake Decorating Made Easy, so I think that title will work just fine.

Part 2: Planning your Video

Now comes a very important step. You can't just go straight to creating a video without a plan.

My video will be 60 seconds long. I want people to get excited enough to find out more information, and they will find out more by going to my website.

So the video should create the need for them to go to my website. If they are interested in Cake Decorating they will be viewing my video because of it, and if I tell them there is a really nice website talking about cake decorating, they will be more likely to visit it.

My video will start with a question, then it will display some really nice cake decorating images, then I will introduce more text as well as more images, another question, more images, another exclamation, more images and finally I will invite the viewer to visit my website.

Do you love Cake Decorating?
I do too!
Have you checked out my free and really awesome techniques?
I know you will like them!
Watch me at CakeDecoratingMadeEasy.net

People get emotional watching videos, and if you touch on their likes, and you share that you have the same likes as them - that will emotionally connect them with you.

Besides that, people like free stuff. Also what cake decorating lovers look for are ideas so they can improve their own cake decorating at home.

Next, be confident that your information will be helpful to your audience and finally, you must tell them specifically what they should do.

That will create curiosity and they will want to visit your website.

This is just a short example. You can create longer videos of course. But remember the importance of creating a plan before taking action.

Ideas are important. Organized ideas will give you a clear vision and applying organized ideas will literally give you great results.

Part 3: Searching for images or video clips

Now you will start looking for the material you will be using in order to create your video.

You can create a video with only text, you can also create it with text and images, and you can even create it with text, images and video clips.

In this case we will use text and images.

So right now we will need several images related to cake decorating. I know it's extremely easy to find great images, but most of them are paid. What I will do is show you how you can save money on images, finding free ones.

Firstly, go to Google, type your keyword and click Search. And then you will select images.

Now, a very important thing to consider here is you can't just pick those images and start using them because many of them might be copyright protected.

So you will refine your search by clicking on Options and Advanced Search.

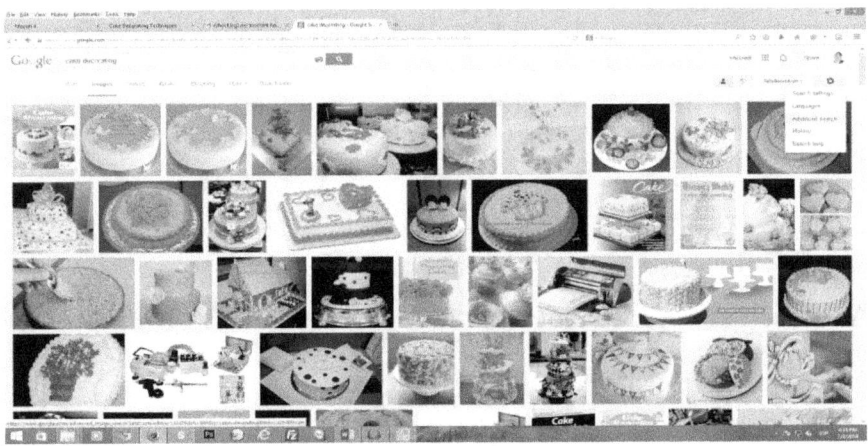

Then you will go down and select "free to use or share even commercially" on the "usage rights" tab. And click Advanced Search.

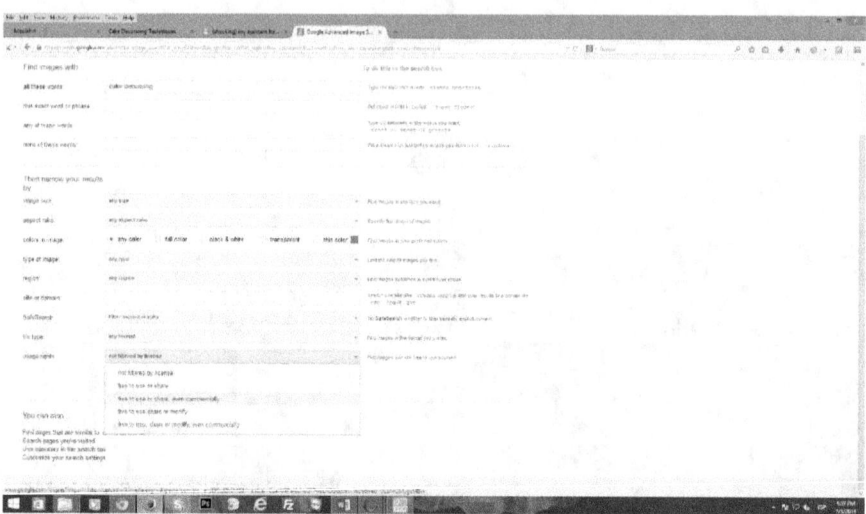

Now you can pick some really nice images and use them without any copyright problems.

Other places you can find free images are the following:

✓ http://www.dreamstime.com/free-photos

✓ https://www.graphicstock.com/freeimages/

✓ http://www.freeimages.com/

✓ http://www.morguefile.com/

✓ http://pixabay.com/

And what about free video clips? Here you have a nice place for that too:

✓ http://www.videoblocks.com/freeclips

Of course it will be a lot better if you use your own images and video clips, but this is an option if you don't have any good looking images and videos.

Part 4: Creating your video

Now the fun part begins. Here I will show you how to create a really nice looking video for dirt cheap.

I will be using a fabulous service called Animoto.

Animoto is one of the greatest *video creation services (online and mobile) that makes it easy and fun for anyone to create and share extraordinary videos using their own pictures, video clips, words and music.*

Millions of people actively use Animoto for everything from special occasions like birthdays, weddings and trips, to sending a quick special greeting, or just to share everyday moments. Taken from Animoto

Animoto has recently launched their Business area. You will be shocked with what you could achieve there. But I would like to show you how to create as many excellent and high quality videos as you want for only $5 with Animoto.

Firstly, you will need to create a brand new account by clicking on "Sign Up."

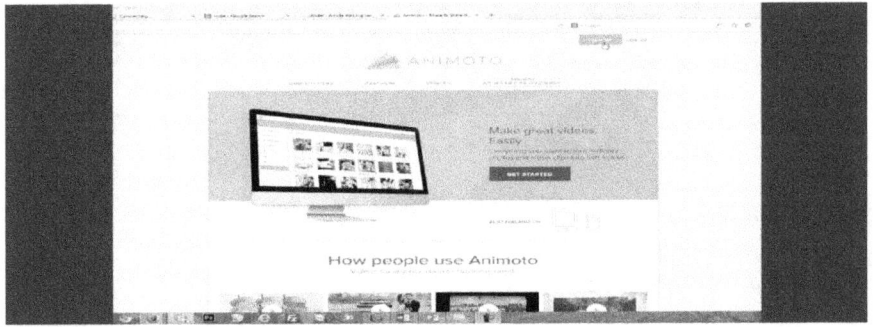

Then you will fill out all your personal details and click on "Sign Up."

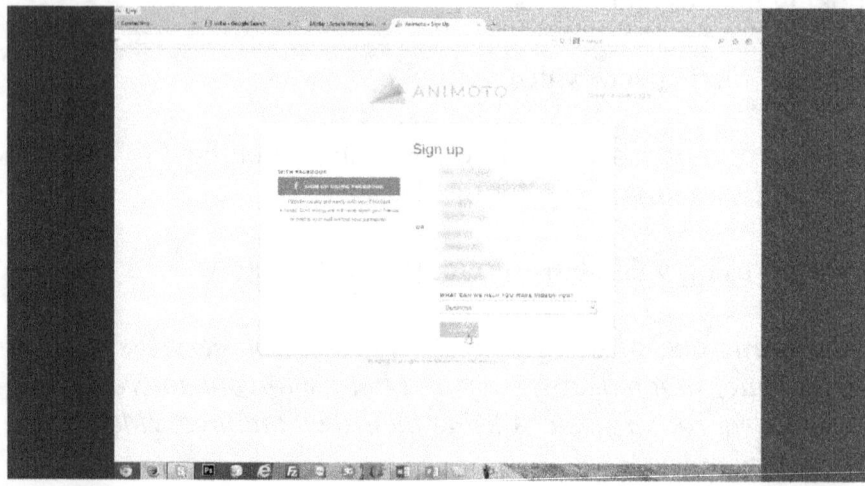

Once inside you will click on the account tab.

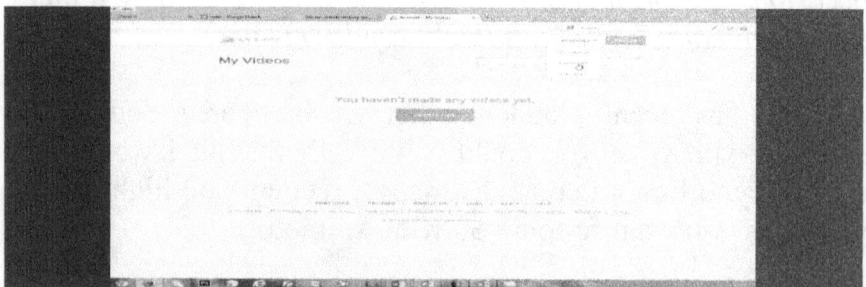

Once there you will upgrade your account.

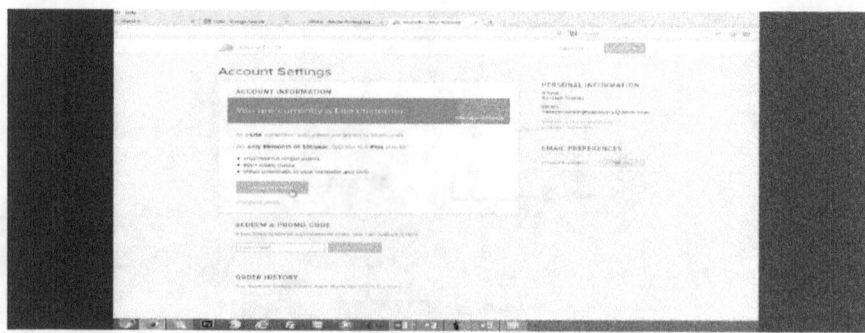

Then you will click right here where it says "See personal pricing plans."

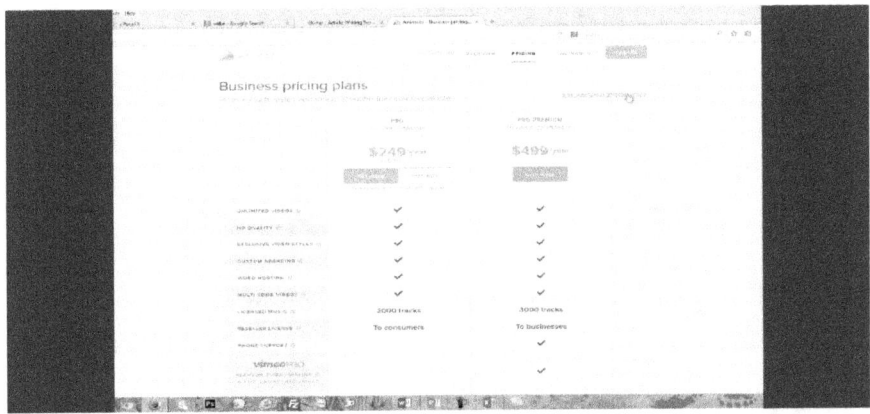

And here is where I want you to look. Pick the PLUS pricing plan, which will be more than enough right now.

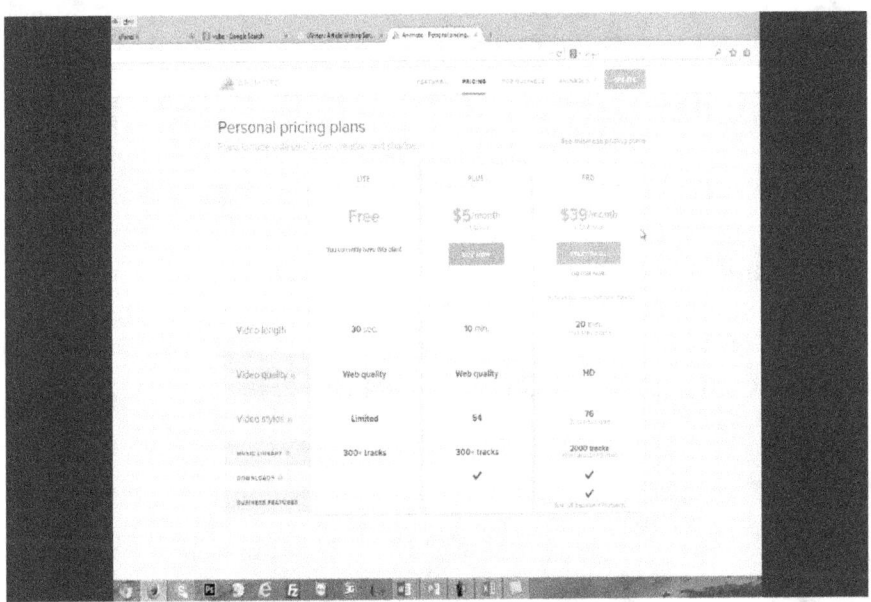

Great, after you have made your payment, you will go over to the "My Videos" Tab and you will see no video has been created. So let's create one now

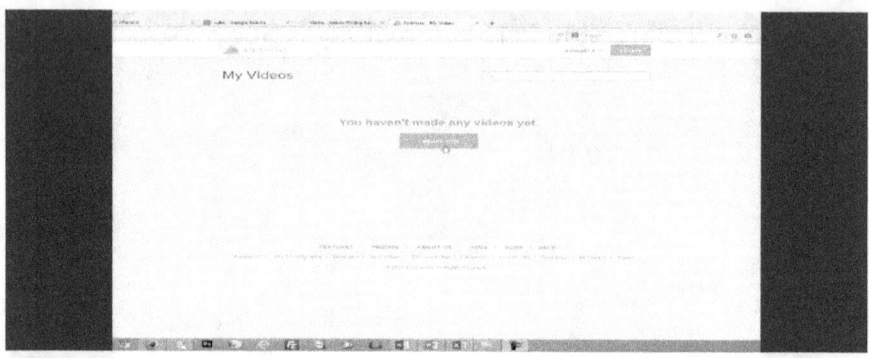

You will be able to choose a style. You can even see a preview of the style. And then you will end up in the Creating dashboard.

This area is extremely easy to manage. You will be able to add pictures and even video clips. You will be able to add text. And afterwards, you will be able to watch a Preview. You will even be able to change the music if you want.

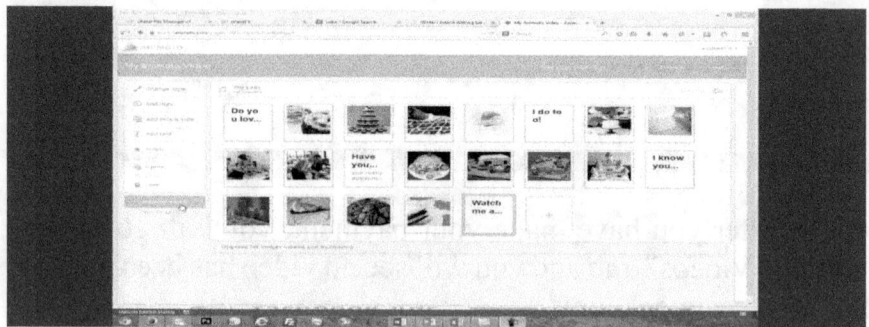

Part 5: Downloading your video

Now that your video is ready, you will be able to download it. But before that, there are a few options you can pick from.

Something very important to consider in the creation process of a video is the quality of the video.

Here with Animoto, you will be able to upgrade the resolution of your video. I recommend you upgrade it to the 720p HD resolution. There is something viewers, including me, really hate about videos, and that is low definition videos.

High definition videos will look original and top quality.

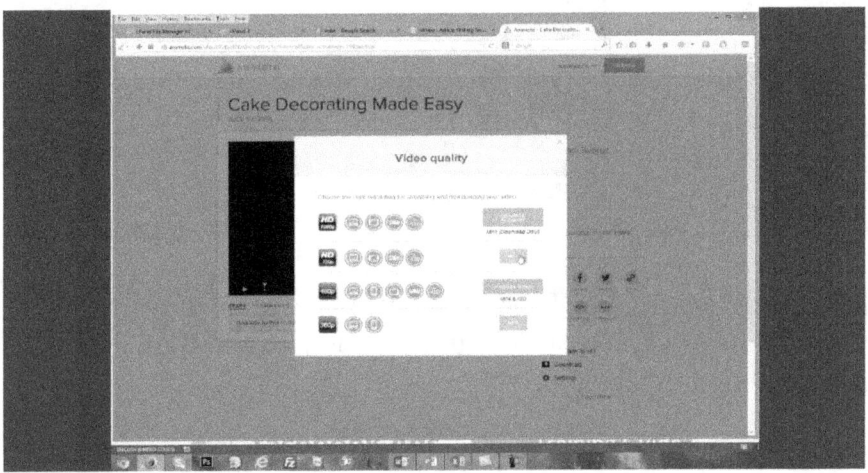

Great, now you are able to download your HD video.

Step 2: Upload

Now I will show you the second step of the process which is uploading your Video.

As you already noticed, there are several video sharing sites where you could upload your video, but I will focus only on one, which is the most important one. YouTube will bring you the greatest benefits in terms of Video Marketing.

In order to upload your brand new video to YouTube, you will need to create a channel.

Creating a YouTube Channel is extremely simple. Firstly, you must go to YouTube.com and Sign in.

In order to create a YouTube Channel on any topic of your choice, you first have to have a YouTube Account, as well as a Google account, already created.

I already have a Google account as well as a YouTube Account. So I will log in. And then you will go to the top right corner and go to the Settings area.

And clicking here, you will be able to see all of your YouTube Channels listed.

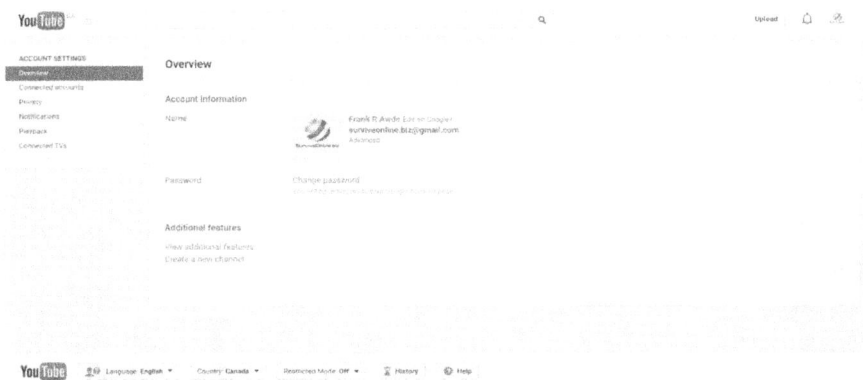

You see I just have one YouTube Channel listed, which is the default channel created when I created the YouTube Account. Now I will create a new one. To do that I will need to click on "Create a new Channel."

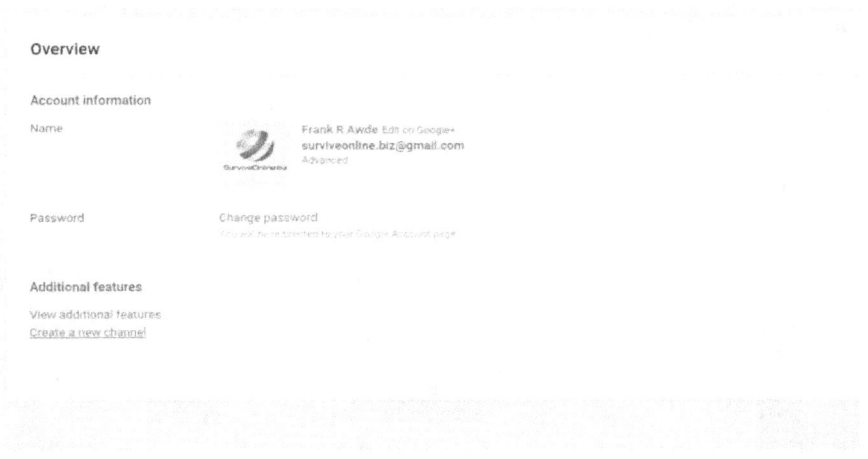

Now something very important for you to do right after creating your brand new YouTube Channel is to put some color into it.

Don't make the common mistake of leaving your YouTube

Channel empty with nothing to see. You will need to at least insert your Channel Icon and your Channel Art.

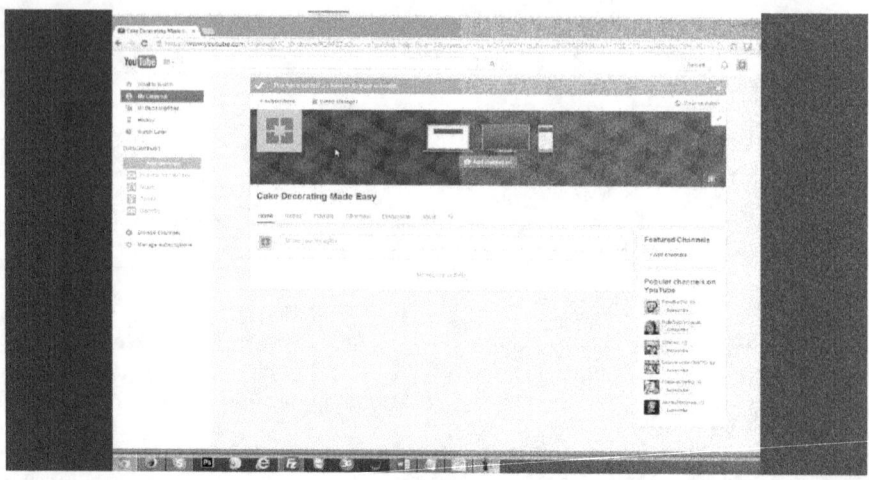

In order to add your Channel Icon, you will be redirected to the Google+ Account of your YouTube Channel. Once you create your YouTube Channel, a new Google+ Account is created at the same time. That happens with every YouTube Channel you create.

The Channel Icon must be at least 250 pixels wide and 250 pixels tall.

The Channel art will be uploading directly to the YouTube Channel. The Channel Art must be at least 2048 pixels wide and 1152 pixels tall.

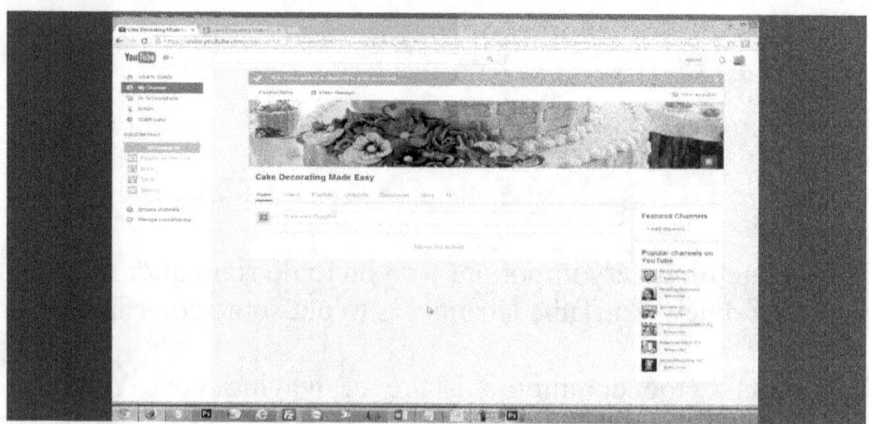

Awesome, your brand new YouTube Channel looks a lot better now. And finally it's time to make it look a lot cooler by uploading your first video.

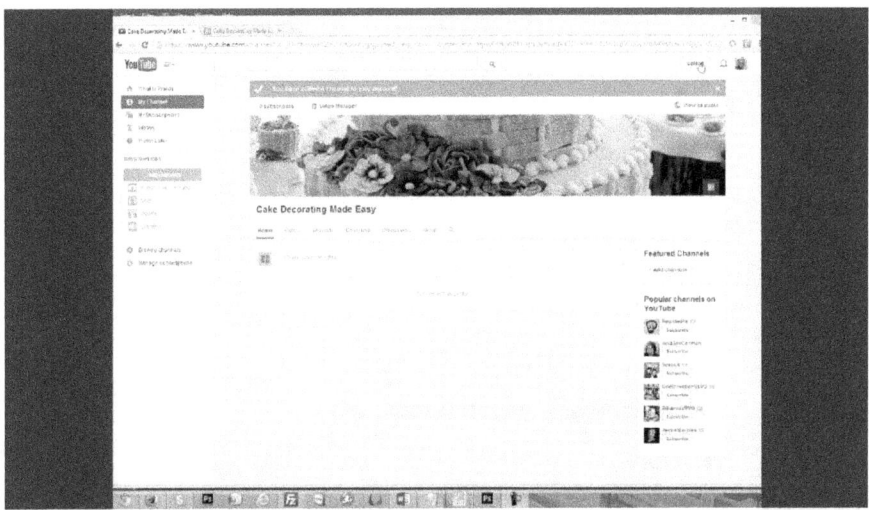

A very important piece of advice before uploading your video is changing the name of the file, so it will display the proper name inside of YouTube.

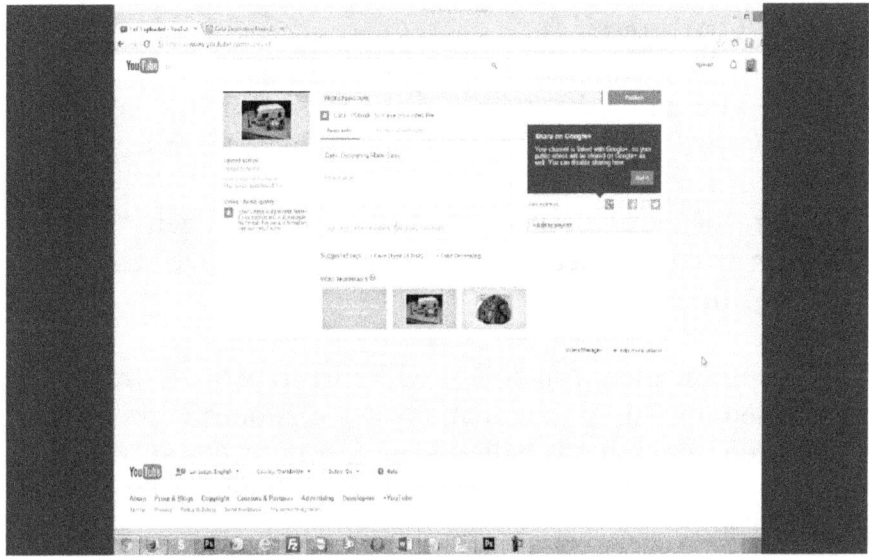

Awesome, your video is uploaded. Now the last thing you will do is to publish it and you are finished.

And this is how your brand new video looks…

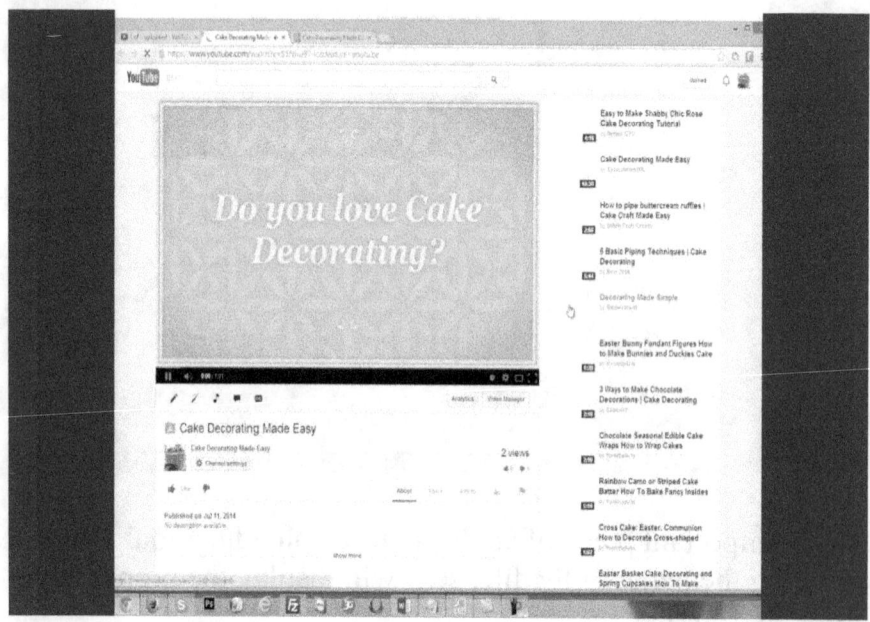

Step 3: Optimize

I'm sure you now think your video will start getting a million views because your topic is hot, but that's not how it works.

In order for your brand new video to start getting some attention from people, you will need to optimize it in some very specific ways.

These optimization principles will direct people straight to your video, but more than that, these techniques will optimize your video with what is called Search Engine Optimization or SEO, so you can get the real traffic we are looking for: Search Engine Traffic

There are two major optimization principles. The first is called ON-Page SEO and the second one is called OFF-Page SEO.

- **ON-Page SEO**

On-page SEO consists of optimizing your video so Search Engines can **"Pick it up and Rank it"**.

There are 4 important On-Page optimization techniques to be aware of:

1. **Your Custom Channel URL:** here on YouTube you will be able to create a unique address URL for your YouTube channel. Besides looking really nice for people to click and visit your YouTube Channel, that URL will also have Search Engine power to get ranked while people perform a related search, especially on Google.

2. **The Title:** as we previously mentioned on Step 1. You must build a title where your business and a hot keyword can be combined. As you already saw, mine is Cake Decorating Made Easy, which is the name of my business and it has a really hot keyword in it.

3. **The Description:** in the description you will be able to include 3 very important things: first you will include your website URL at the top; secondly you will include a very nice description where you will mention the hot keyword 4 times, and lastly, you will include your YouTube Custom Channel URL at the bottom of your description.

4. **The Tags:** Here you will be able to insert as many keyword variations as possible. You can just type anything that comes to your mind. You can even use the Google Keyword Planner for more ideas.

Now your brand new YouTube Video looks a lot better.

- **OFF-Page SEO**

Off-page SEO consists of applying some link building techniques from other websites to your Video, so search engines can **"FIND"** your video a lot faster.

This is not about buying views; this is about making your video a lot more FINDABLE for the search engines.

Before applying the following optimization techniques, you have to make sure you know what your YouTube Video URL is, as you don't want to be working hard advertising the wrong URL.

My YouTube Video URL looks like this:

https://www.youtube.com/watch?v=S5NIxuB7-ic

Yours will probably look similar.

There are 5 important Off-Page optimization techniques to be aware of:

1. Get organic views to your YouTube Video URL by using YouLikeHits.com, which consists of a promotional tool that will help you grow your Twitter, MySpace, YouTube, Google+, StumbleUpon, Pinterest, SoundCloud and Websites for FREE.

2. Build Social Bookmarks to your YouTube Video URL: there are so many ways to do this nowadays. I advise you to hire someone from Fiverr.com. Make sure to take a look at what people say about the service you are about to pay for, read the reviews.

3. Take your YouTube Video URL and all of the Bookmarks you built on it and submit them at Linklicious.co

4. Take your YouTube Video URL and all of the Bookmarks you built on it and submit them at Mass-ping.com.

5. For more ranking power, build WIKI Links to your YouTube Video URL. Get help at Fiverr.com for this.

Now you just need to wait until your video gets ranked in the top search engine results. It might take days, even a few weeks.

But if for some reason it doesn't, you might need to apply more Off-Page optimization, because maybe there are other marketers like you applying the same techniques you are applying for the exact same keyword on a different video.

Step 4: Advertise

There is always a way to automate anything on the web, and the same is true with traffic to your video.

There are other ways you could advertise your video, but you have to remember that the real intention of your video is to make people do something, take action.

• **Social Advertising**

There are many ideas you could use to make your video go viral, and one of the greatest ones is posting on social websites.

Maybe you are trying to get people to visit your website or an affiliate product. You might be asking yourself, why don't I just post my website URL or affiliate links directly to my social accounts like Facebook or Twitter, instead of sending them a video that will redirect them to your website or URL? There are many reasons for this, but the strongest ones are:

1. **Not all social platforms allow you to post all kinds of**

URLs. Some social platforms really hate marketers placing CPA offers on their posts. Even the CPA owners don't allow that, and the way you might find out if that's true is doing it and getting your account shut down, and because you don't want that happen to you, just don't do it. So that's why it is recommended to post a video redirecting them to your offer. You could buy a relevant domain name and have it redirected to your CPA or Affiliate offer.

2. **People react differently**. People's attention to a video will be a lot more positive and attractive than just looking at a URL. People love watching videos, people like to hang out on social media. Even I don't read a single word of what people type on their social accounts, I love to WATCH the videos. Twitter is a great example of this. They limit your post to a maximum number of characters because people don't take the time to read too much.

3. **It prepares them to act.** The purpose of a video is preparing the viewer so once he enters your website or clicks on your affiliate link, he is already prepared to do something. That would be what is called high converting or warm traffic. Cold traffic would be if you just post your link there and then they go straight to a sales page.

4. **It could go viral.** If people love your video they will comment on it, they may retweet it, they can share it, they will do something with it, and that's the power of social media. With just a click your video can go wildly viral.

Those are the most important reasons for posting your video on social media.

•   **Sponsored Advertising**

Something awesome about several video sharing sites is that

they offer special advertising services for your video. This is how movie companies prelaunch their latest Blockbusters before they go live to the public.

You normally will find their advertising section at the bottom of their website.

Some of them offer a special section of success stories where you are able to see what results other businesses are getting and how they are doing it. That is extremely helpful for any business that wants to venture into this awesome advertising solution.

Others let you place your video on different parts of the video display area, like next to another video already playing, or as a related video option, or in the sponsor video section. You can even have them contact you and prepare an awesome video marketing campaign that will bring some seriously great results.

As you can see, anything is possible with video. Just think of another idea, search it on the web and I'm sure you will find that idea already has a service waiting for you to use.

Chapter 7
Highly Effective Video Marketing Tricks

- **Add a Call-to-Action Overlay:**

Overlay is a banner advertisement which appears at the start of a video.

You can install it if you are using YouTube. You have complete control over your copy, the thumbnail image, and the landing page where you want to send the traffic. If you forget to do this, you will surely lose valuable traffic.

- **Ask viewers to act**

When you create a video, guide your customer, tell them what the next thing is they should do.

If you don't invite them to do something, that's exactly what they will do: nothing. If you want them to click on something, tell them. If you want them to buy, ask them. You must invite them to act. Your videos are really there to get them to take action.

- **Add the Description of your Video**

This is very important and a lot of people don't do it. Every time you upload a video, you have to take advantage of the opportunity to describe the video content. With this you have the chance to add more calls to action. This is another key area for ranking your video in the top of the search engines. Google crawls YouTube descriptions.

- **Add the URL in the Description Box**

I know this may sound obvious, but I have to remind you to do this. Every time you upload a video, don't miss the chance to insert your website address or any URL you want. Take advantage of the high converting power of your video.

You can invite people to visit your website from the video itself, but a lot of people including myself, are too lazy to type a URL, so we decide to go to the description box and click on the URL.

- **Include a real person**

Including a real person in your video increases audience trust in your brand. It will put a face to your brand. You can show them how passionate you are about your product. You can take a look at how other important Internet Marketers show their faces to everyone. This builds an amazing personal brand, because next time they see your name, they will know who you are.

- **Post videos regularly**

People have to see you are alive. After some time, people will start wondering why you don't post new videos. It implies you don't care about them.

Post videos on a regular basis. The cool thing about videos is that people will watch them, it is much more appealing than reading a text post.

- **Address a trendy topic**

Of course you can't just post boring information. You must provide quality every single time you post a new video. If you don't know what to post, just research about the latest information on your niche and say some useful stuff about it.

You can even email them asking what topics they would like to learn about the most. You can even take a look at the emails they send you and record a video answering all of their inquiries. This will make very happy customers or clients.

- **Video Apologies**

Video apologies work awesome. If there is something people are having a hard time with regarding your product or service on a normal basis, use a video as an apology for that.

If for some reason there was a mistake related to anything in your business, just take the time to say sorry. When business owners do that, it will increase the customers trust in them. This shows you care about them.

- **Interactive Videos are what people want**

Please do not just talk. Try to make the video attractive, funny and easy to understand. People love to see live examples of something.

Show them live how to use your product. Show them live how to resolve an issue. Show them live what people are saying about your product or services as well. Showing how they are using your product or services is all a great strategy.

*   **Enjoy what you do**

Be enthusiastic, be funny, be their friend, feel happy recording a new video, and they will feel the same way watching it.

Chapter 8
The Hottest Ways to use Video for Marketing

- **Website Traffic**

With the help of a video you can direct people to any website you want. You can direct traffic to your domain name and to any part of your website.

You can even place a list of useful URLs where people can get the information you are advertising with your video.

- **Affiliate Marketing**

Internet marketers use videos to direct people straight to affiliate offers by using a personalized affiliate URL, so they can make commissions for any sale generated.

Something commonly used is a URL shortener like Bitly.com and Ow.ly to make their ugly and strange affiliate URL friendlier to users.

- **CPA Marketing**

Same as with affiliate offers, Internet marketers use videos to direct people straight to CPA offers by using a personalized affiliate URL, so they can make commissions for any action taken.

Actions could be like submitting a zip code, submitting an email, taking a free trial, etc.

- **Lead Generation**

Videos are an awesome way to build a subscribers list. Sending people to a landing page, or to what is known as a squeeze page where people can receive something they are interested in by submitting their email is the common way to do it. You can offer a free video, report, software, training, webinar, etc.

- **Training**

You can't provide personal training for every new employee or even customer that comes to your company, so video is the easiest and best way to achieve this. It saves you time and cost. You don't have to pay again and again for the same training. People love to learn stuff live, they want to know how to use the product, and there is no better way for this than video.

- **Webinars**

Webinars are one of the greatest ways to make big money on the web by selling high priced training courses. The presenter shows live how the product works, and then shows some proof of the benefits of the product.

Then after a live, real and proven demonstration, it sells the product. The viewer is definitely sure it is going to work for him too.

- **Customer Service**

Video also helps you to teach your employees "how to treat your customers". You have to create a step by step video to make them understand customer's problems. This will increase your employee's work efficiency. You can even create Specialized

Training Videos for common problems customers will find while using your product or services.

- **Updates**

Maybe there are some very important updates on a specific part or on several sections of your business. You can just create a few videos about it instead of redoing the whole training.

Internet Marketing Experts launch the exact same product several times and call it Version 2 or Version 3, but what they do is update some videos and create new ones so the process perfectly fits to actual updates of the website or tools the product owner uses to offer his service.

- **Sales Pages**

You can visit every single sales page on the web and I'm sure 9 out of 10 of them will have a video right on top of it. Videos grab the visitors' attention quickly. People love to see videos, and if the video is interesting enough, they will watch it until the end.

When was the last time you read a sales page from start to finish? I never have done that myself. People hate to read on the web, because the web is so fast and so huge, they just want to jump from one page to another. People don't read the Internet, people navigate the Internet.

- **Upsell Offers**

Same as on Sale Pages, videos are commonly used on upsell offers. If people don't read Front End Offers they probably won't read upsell offers. The upsell offer is a lot shorter than the Front End offer because people are already in what is called a buying mood. They won't need a lot of convincing in this part but they will need a very specific video about what else you have for them to get faster and better results with your product or service.

Chapter 9
Video Marketing Case Studies

Here are some case studies that use video marketing as their tool to increase their conversions. These stories will inspire you to think more creatively as well as show you can do video marketing with any local businesses.

- **ZAGG**

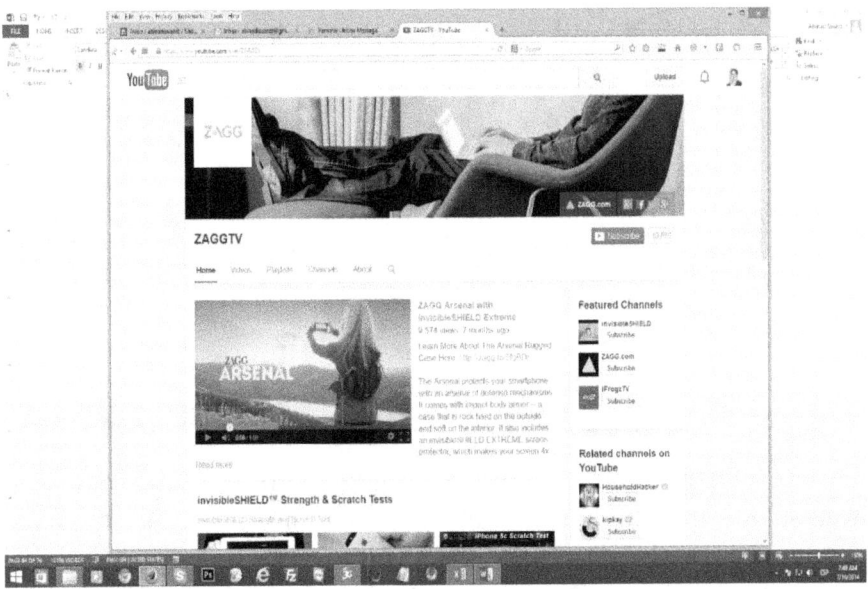

Zagg is an innovator of scratch-protection and accessories for portable devices like device protection solutions, including shields, skins, cases and many more. Zagg engages and educates its customers using the power and flexibility of video.

Drew Conrad, internet marketing specialist for Zagg said, "There's really no other way we can get such personally meaningful video content in front of so many eyes. YouTube video ads have boosted our search traffic, and we're enjoying the largest surge in sales that we've ever seen".

They want to drive traffic with videos and ads, attract new customers, and educate their viewers about how the invisible shield works. They got 13 million views on their branded YouTube channel for a specific product. And targeted video increased their conversion rate by 75%.

- **Undercover Tourist**

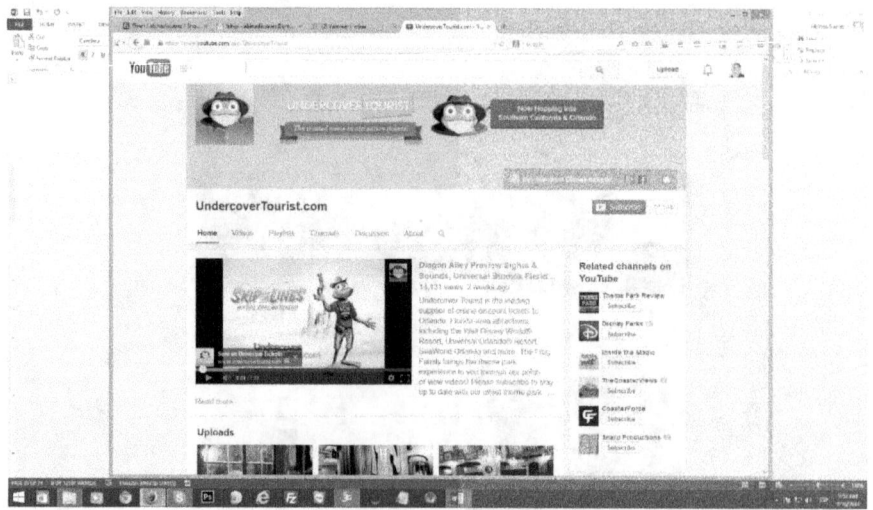

This is a Disney Park in the US. The problem with the park was issuing genuine park tickets in a safe and timely manner, eliminating the frustration of standing in lines to redeem a voucher at the gate. They wanted to improve the quantity of qualified sales leads.

Ian Ford, CEO for Undercover Tourist said, "Our formula on YouTube video is simple and effective. We shoot authentic, point-of-view, un-slick content with a steady hand and slow pans. We engage people with the experience itself rather than overwhelm them with a corporate voice."

They uploaded authentic, short, POV videos to educate visitors. They got 10 million views with an increase of 3-5% in click through.

- **BerkleeMusic**

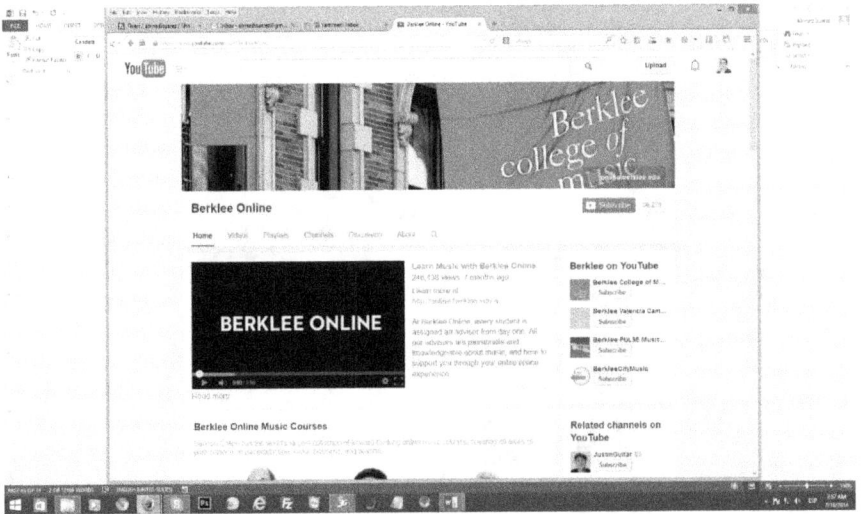

BerkleeMusic is the award-winning online school of Berklee College of Music. It has the largest collection of forward-thinking online courses for music production and performance.

They want to increase their music exposure to world-class courses in music and boost enrollment in their online school. To reach their goal they consistently improve video production levels, and build synergistic marketing strategy by combining various channels.

The result of this music school was incredible. Raymond says, "Our branded YouTube channel has 300 videos, reaches more than 33,500 subscribers, and has garnered 16.7 million video views". It became the 5th most viewed educational channel on YouTube.

Milan Kovacev, director of interactive marketing for BerkleeMusic says, "We have created several 15-second video ads for our latest YouTube video advertising campaign. Using great demographic and marketing tools available in AdWords on our recruitment and marketing goals".

- **Frontpoint Security**

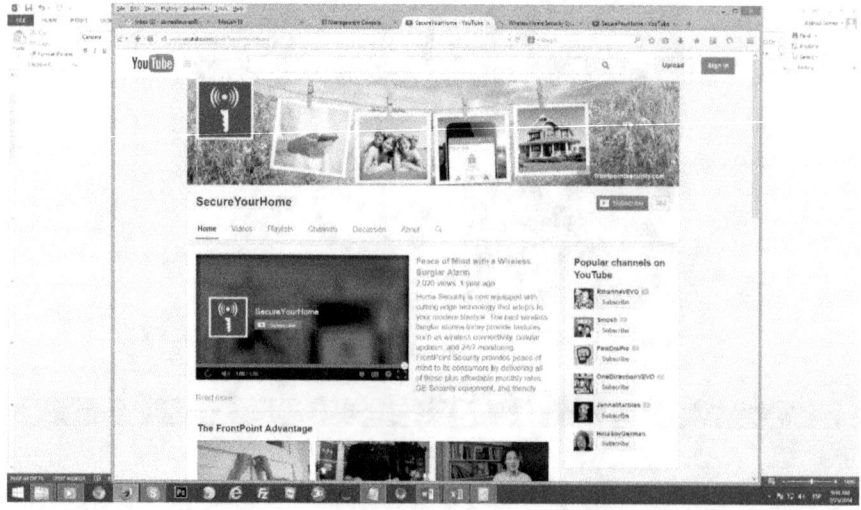

Frontpoint Security is a home security company which provides wireless alarm sensors, DIY security and a unique cellular link providing unmatched protection.

This security company is facing the problem of how to explain their user friendly security systems benefits. So they went to YouTube and created a 2 minute video with their product demonstration. These videos work very well and their sales increased by 250% - and they also generate thousands of views.

- **Global Fire Creative**

Global Fire Creative is a UK based production company which works with a number of global brands and organizations. This company uses Vimeo as a tool to connect with their clients.

They tell about their products and services with Vimeo video and also create Vimeo video for their client's services. To give a professional look, they created different videos for Vimeo, according to the clients' demands.

They use video for clients' success stories as a strong, emotive way to take current customers and pair them up with their future ones for a bond that communicates, "You can trust us. We love this product and we're real people."

- **Sony – Xperia play**

Sony wants to create buzz on the web and also establish a gaming world with the <u>Xperia Play Smartphone</u>. The brand planned a viral campaign to reach targeted people between 25-35 years old.

<u>DailyMotion</u> planned a global event to make it viral. It used Buzzing videos, released editorials, displayed in-stream ads to announce to and interact with their customers. The sharable features were also useful in this campaign.

As a result, they got 7 million views on Dailymotion, more than 13k likes on Facebook and more than 200 tweets. This campaign was also spread on blogs.

- **Issey Miyake**

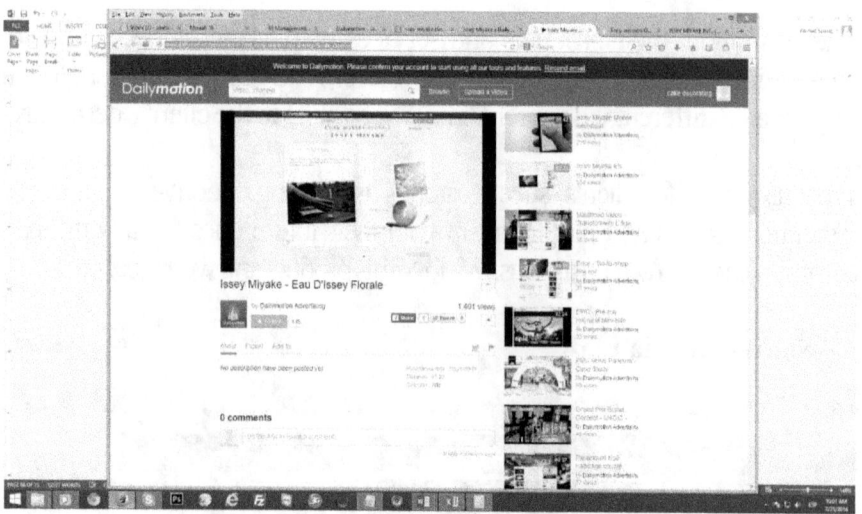

<u>Issey Miyake</u> is a Japanese fashion designer, and he is known for his technology-driven clothing designs, exhibitions, watches, and fragrances.

Issey Miyake used DailyMotion video marketing to provide a purely emotional experience to target young women.

Issey Miyake perfume brand "L'Eau d'Issey" wanted to create an emotional experience for their targeted women.

The result was they got 300,000 video views on the official page. The targeted audience is immersed in the brand atmosphere with emotional interactivity and displays on the website and via mobile.

- **Sara Lee Corporation**

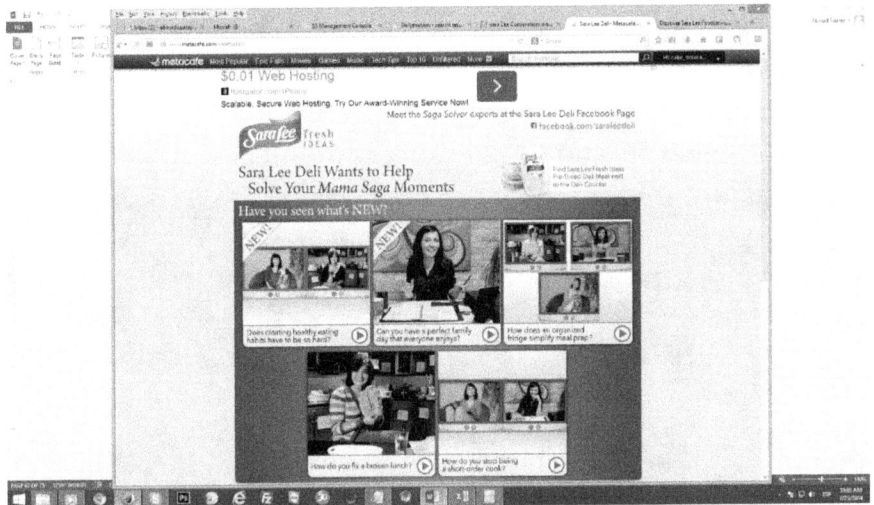

The Sara Lee Corporation is an American consumer-goods Company based in Downers Grove, Illinois. It's also an iconic food brand. It launched its first big social media campaign and created three mom-centric viral videos to push their marketing strategy.

The challenges were in finding the right way to be viewed and getting the clip to the right audience. No one can just predict what video will go viral.

Robert Davis, leader of the online video practice at Ogilvy said, "Metacafe has been out-performing other shared video sites when it comes to search shelf space, which made us sit up and take notice".

"We broke through the million-view mark in a matter of weeks. As much as we like to profess we understand this business, and we do, it's really fun when a marketer comes across new assets that might not be so predictable."

Metacafe built a channel for this corporation including one video of the trio mom confessional videos. They got more than 800 k views and their revenue was up 50% with Metacafe from the last year.

• **Welch Foods Inc. (Welch's)**

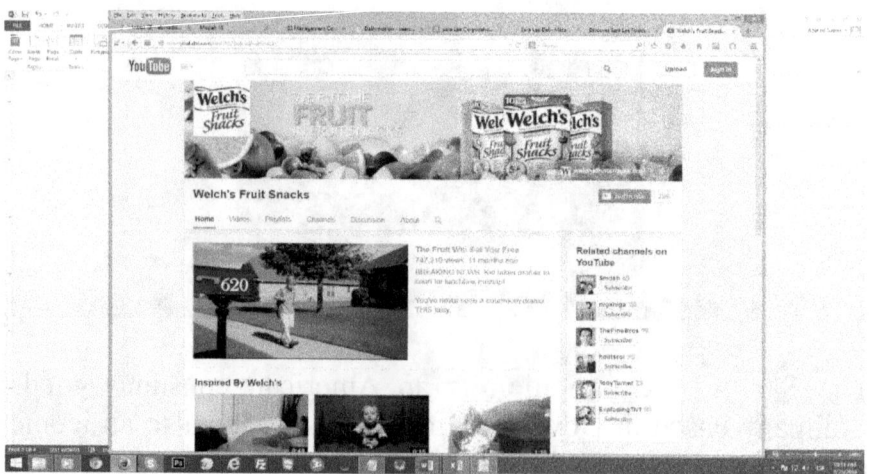

Welch's is the food processing and marketing arm of the National Grape Cooperative Association.

To increase their brand awareness and product promotion in the UK market, they used video marketing with YouTube, Vimeo and other channels to increase their brand reputation.

They also targeted their TV viewers with a Healthy Heart Week

Sponsorship Video campaign on GMTV. They connected images and sounds of the heart with glasses of the product, in video. They also included their product information and benefits in video.

Video marketing increased their sales by 75% in the first year and 35% in the next year.

- **Charles Smith**

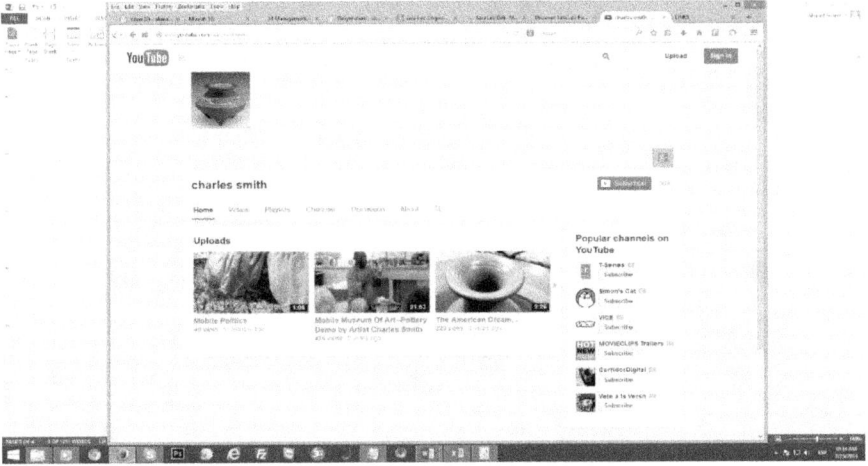

Since Charles Smith, who is from Atlanta, Georgia, started marketing his pottery business using videos, he does not need to travel into town to get orders for his art at galleries and fairs.

When he transitioned to video marketing, through his videos he found new buyers from around the world. This saved him time and money which he was spending in travelling. He includes in his video, how to create art and galleries. He is blowing people away. Viewers are amazed watching him do his art.

Chapter 10

What to Do and What not to Do

Do's:

✓ **Invite your audience:** Mention a clear call to action in the video to deploy and engage your potential audience. You can create a campaign with a clear message to invite them.

✓ **Keep it short:** There are so many other websites of competitors in your market that can grab your audience's attention. Most people like to watch a video only about 90 seconds in length. Short video forces you to simplify your message, it encourages engagement, reflects your business positively and increases your video quality.

✓ **Humanize your brand:** When people interact with a real face in a video, it increases the trust factor and puts a brand to your face. Humanizing your brand is a big win for you. It will enable you to make great connections with your viewers.

✓ **Title is important:** The title is the first impression of your videos. Your video should have the relevant information which you mention in the title. Video titles also can pull in traffic. Attractive and meaningful titles can grab the viewer's attention instantly. It will make your video easily found on search engines. Titles should describe your video, contain the keyword, and be short and sweet.

✓ **Optimize:** You are going to upload your videos on multiple sites, so here you need to create a particular description and title for each video. You should have a goal before creating the video, include a call to action to follow up your leads, and add a lead capturing method with your videos.

✓ **Sharable:** Make sure your video is engaging and compelling so that your audience will share this with their friends and family on social media and other channels. This will work as an extra edge for your business, and will give you more exposure.

✓ **Be creative:** Be more creative with your videos. Think of new ideas to describe your product and services, which helps you get new customers. And you will get a better return on your investment. Your video should be different and unique from others.

✓ **Add video to your post:** You can add video to your blog posts and social media posts to increase traffic to your video. You can link that video to your website to increase your conversion rates.

✓ **Analyze your performance:** Tracking your video's performance is an integral aspect of a video marketing campaign. See what viewers are saying about you, how many people like your videos, and what comments you get for your video. These things will tell you what you need to change or improve in your next videos.

✓ **Describe your videos:** Don't forget to describe each and every video; a rich description of your videos is a must to get more views. You can use hash tags and your website URL in your description. Hash tags in a description will help your viewers find your video on social platforms.

Don'ts:

✓ **Don't follow a set formula:** Videos fail to engage audiences if you take a formulaic approach. You have to look and think differently for each video. You don't know when a new magic trick will work for your brand.

✓ **Don't forget to define purpose:** Ask yourself why you need to create this video? This will help you define the purpose to your viewers. Defining purpose is a marketing strategy to promote products and services.

✓ **Don't pitch:** If you create a short video of around 1-2 minute with a sales pitch, then people will not be interested in watching your videos. They will go elsewhere.

✓ **Don't forget to include a call to action:** If you didn't use a call to action throughout your entire video, it will harm you. Include a call to action in your video to engage them.

✓ **Don't create just one video:** Creating one video is not enough. You can create many versions of it and you can check which one is working for you. Replace the old video with the new one that is working for your targeted audience.

✓ **Don't ignore sound quality:** Video is much more than just visual content. Visual content can't work alone. You have to add video and audio content to make it stronger. You can improve the quality of video by positioning the mic correctly and choosing the right music for your video.

✓ **Don't include too many messages:** If you have included too many messages in your videos, it will confuse your audience, and they won't know what is useful for them.

You need to have a strong message you want to tell your audience.

✓ **Don't forget to use SEO:** Just uploading your video online is not enough to get expected traffic. You can optimize your video with SEO. SEO will enhance your chances of being found in search engine rankings. You can use keywords in your title for better search results.

✓ **Don't expect instant results:** You upload your video on your online video channel and now you're expecting more views instantly. Well, you should be patient. Market your video on other channels and social media. Your work and patience will eventually pay off for you.

✓ **Don't try to focus on everyone:** You should focus on your target market. Everyone has different interests, so don't try to focus on everyone. If you are doing that, then you are taking a risk that NO ONE will want to view your video. Focus on your target market.

Chapter 11
Creating Videos - Tools and Tricks

The first and most important aspect of video marketing is being able to create high quality and professional-looking videos to represent your business.

If you're unable to do this, then you may not engage your audience and you won't be able to show yourself as a business that they can trust to provide quality work.

Remember, the aim here is to show that your organization is highly capable and has great attention to detail.

The presumption will be that the quality of your video is indicative of the quality of your service or products, so ensure that your viewers are blown away by your production values.

The only real challenge is that most of us aren't James Cameron and if you have a small business, you might not have the resources, time or the skills to create videos that can compete with larger organizations.

Not to worry. With the right strategy, it's possible for anyone to create a video that evokes quality and has the desired effect.

Let's look at some strategies you can use to instantly increase the production values of your videos and impress your audience.

Bear in mind that not all of these tips are going to be relevant in every case – different types of marketing video may have different requirements.

Video Quality

If you're filming the video yourself and you need it to contain footage rather than static images, then make sure that it uses high quality footage.

This means, paying attention to resolution, frame rate and sound quality.

➢ Camera

The first step in achieving this is to film at a high resolution with a camera that produces crisp, 720p or higher HD, and well-lit images.

This will generally come down to the quality of your video camera and of course you are likely to be limited by your budget.

That said, there are some surprisingly high quality cameras you can get for a relatively small initial investment.

The GoPro for instance records in 1080p (at least) and offers a wide-angle lens for capturing a lot in a shot.

Likewise, many smartphones these days actually offer incredibly high-res cameras. A great example of this is the Galaxy Note 5 which actually is capable of recording in 4K resolution.

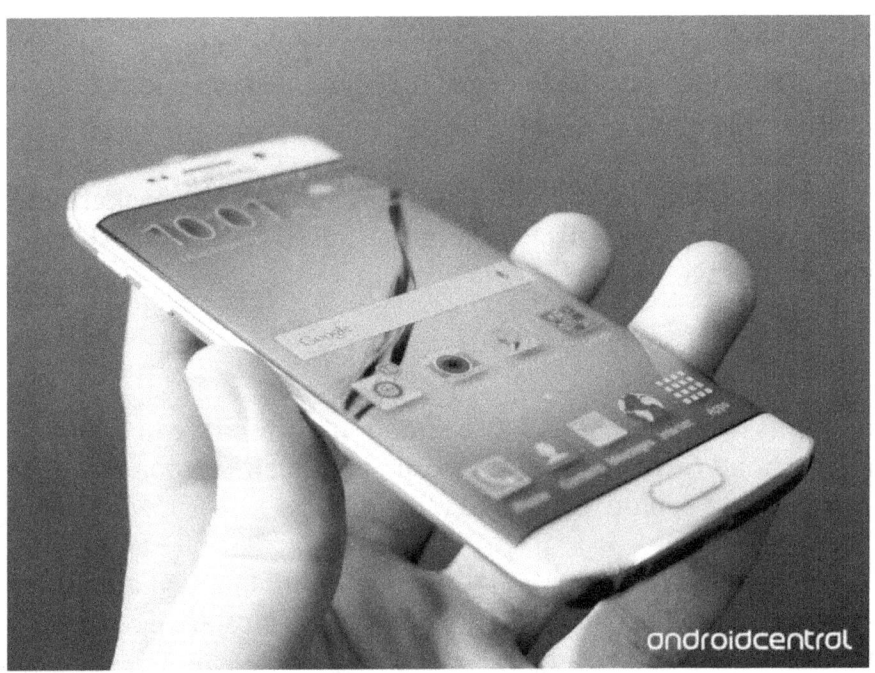

However, if you don't have a high end smartphone and you aren't able to shell out for a GoPro, you may still already have what you need in a
modern SLR camera.

Many, if not most, small SLR and pocket cameras today have the ability to shoot HD video in at least 720p.

If all else fails, then remember you can always ask others to use their devices. Most people should have at least one friend who has a camera that can record in 720p or 1080p – just ask if you can use it for a little while.

Over time, as you start to see returns on your video marketing, you should then be able to invest in more and more equipment to increase the quality of your videos.

Note: that if you want to do things like blur out the background (macros) then you will need a more high-tech camera. Check your camera's features.

➤ Audio

In terms of sound, the ideal situation is to have a separate microphone (lavalier mic) that you can attach to your collar or elsewhere to capture the sound clearly.

If you don't have this option, then make sure that you aren't too far away from the camera and that the acoustics are good in the room that you're filming in.

One highly recommended trick for sound recording, is to record your voice on a smartphone or recorder and download it and sync it to the video when editing.

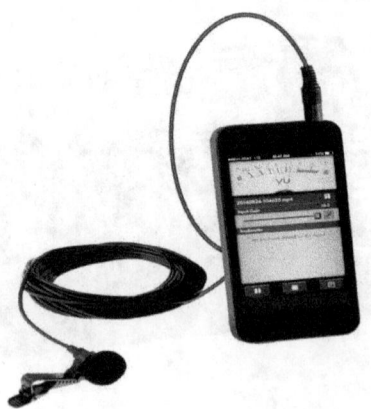

A high ceiling in an empty room can create echoes while a busy environment outside will drown you out and can again make your video seem less professional.

Test, test and test again,

as your sound quality is very important. Videos with poor sound appear unprofessional.

Setting the Scene

Video quality isn't just about the camera. Just as important is making sure that you set the scene and the lighting will play a big part here.

Essentially, you need to ensure that your room is well-lit so that your viewers can see you clearly. This will also impact on the professionalism of the final product.

➤ Lighting

If you are willing to invest a bit more money into your video marketing, then you can always get hold of some professional lighting equipment (called light boxes).

If not, then a desk lamp with an adjustable angle can actually do a surprisingly good job.

Failing that, positioning yourself correctly by a window even is fine. To create the most professional look, you should aim to use 'Rembrandt lighting' which means that half your face will be lit from a 90 degree angle.

This is a little more dramatic and creates depth and contrast in your footage.

You also need to avoid filming with any light sources directly behind the camera which can create glare.

Next, consider the surroundings and what else is in the shot with you.

As we mentioned earlier, a video filmed in your bedroom is hardly going to inspire confidence in your brand so you need to make certain that you have maintained a professional looking environment.

The easiest way to do this is with a completely white backdrop.

A white wall doesn't quite do the trick here though as it will have shadows and won't be completely white – instead you're trying to create the effect of 'infinite white' which should look like you're standing in the middle of nothing.

It is possible to get professional white backdrops but in the interests of keeping your budget low, you can also actually use a bed sheet (pulled taut with some tape or some pegs) or a large piece of white paper.

As long as the light is bright enough and you decrease shadows/ contrast in post-production, this can look surprisingly effective

(and remember to iron that sheet!)

The great thing about filming on infinite white backdrops is that they also give you the most options in your editing, as you'll be able to move the subject around, introduce new elements etc.

Alternatively, you can just choose somewhere 'neutral' for your filming. This could be out in a park somewhere, or it could be walking through town.

These sorts of settings again remove the DIY element by taking you into a setting where people aren't going to see your kids' toys in the background.

Shooting in your place of business can be the best of them all. If you have a shop or physical business location, then your best bet is to shoot your video right in your shop or office.

Finally, you can try creating your own backdrop using other materials.

This might mean organizing some books in the background

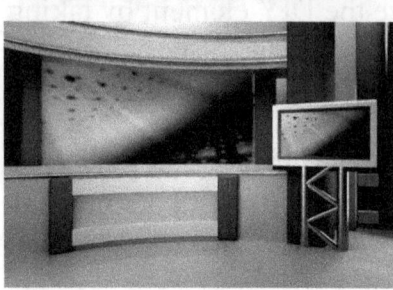

that are about your industry, or it might mean printing out a large poster with your logo on it.

For a more advanced look, you can use green screen or a Chroma key background and digitally add in a background or studio look.

If you're fortunate enough to have a professional looking store or office, then it is acceptable to film from that environment but make sure you tidy up and choose the spot with the best lighting and the most interesting (without being distracting) background.

➤ Presentation

Unfortunately, the majority of us are not natural-born presenters and when you put yourself in-front of the camera, you will quickly see just how hard the job of a television presenter really is.

Not only do you need to look the part, but you also need to deliver your lines confidently and professionally in a way that's engaging and without speech habits like ums and ahs.

If you are shooting lots of takes and find yourself stumbling over your lines, then here are a few tips that can help.

The first is to write yourself a script. Reading your lines will help you to speak much more fluently and with fewer errors but make sure it doesn't sound like you're just reading. Practice and have your script almost memorized.

Using a budget iPad teleprompter is also a great way to stay on script. If you need to read, this is an inexpensive, professional solution.

Another great tip is to have a bullet point list of your topic, posted behind the camera or your interviewer.

You can now stay on topic and sound more natural at the same time.

Engage with the audience by sounding as natural and enthusiastic as if you were talking to your friend about an amazing new business you just found out about.

Another way to avoid bad speech habits is to film in multiple takes. Rather than trying to deliver an entire video in one perfect take, break it down into small chunks and then edit it together.

Almost all professional video and TV sticks with the 10 second rule. 10 to 12 seconds between scenes.

This can be achieved by taking small multi camera shots and editing them together. The more cameras running at the same time on you, the better.

If you watch back any professional video on YouTube, you'll see that they do the same thing and the constant stopping and starting actually aids the overall professional feel.

This can be used to create more emphasis, add to comic timing and keep your audience engaged.

Remember to speak slightly slower than you normally would, (particularly because we tend to speed up when we're nervous), enunciate and be sure to project your voice.

Look your best by wearing attire that is suitable for your video production or business environment.

Your customer may perceive your business and the work you do based on how you look in your video.

Professional casual seems to be a good middle road, but don't be afraid to dress like you would at your place of work. Natural is best.

This may sound like a no-brainer but you'd be surprised how many business owners think it's okay to record their video marketing in an old dirty T-shirt.

Of course, if that is the image your going for, great, but I recommend you keep it as professional as possible.

Remember that if things go well, you are going to be seen by thousands of people, many of whom might become important clients.

Dress like you're going to your most important business meeting.

A little makeup can go a long way too but ask someone who knows what they're doing. You don't want to over do it, but HD video shows every little thing.

➤ Editing

Once you have all your footage, the next step is to edit that into something cohesive and engaging.

Editing can go a long way to making your video much more professional, even if the footage you have isn't perfect.

The most important thing to keep in mind with your editing is that you want to remove pauses and silent spots. No dead air.

Try to ensure that your video has a 'flow' so there aren't any spots where it feels awkward or where it might lose the viewers' attention.

This is another reason you want to break long dialog down and then edit them together to remove gaps. Generally speaking, the more you can cut away from the video, the better it will be. To keep attention, it must keep moving.

Shorter videos tend to be more effective. This is also important for less professional videos that are aimed at a younger audience.

For B2B videos, or commercials, you may want to use a different approach to your editing.

Here, a professional looking technique is to film your script using two or more cameras running at once and set up from different angles.

This way you can cut to a different shot. This means you can create the illusion of a continuous flow of dialogue (rather than having an awkward cut where your position changes slightly).

Changing camera angles also creates more movement in your videos and makes them feel more dynamic as a result.

By using more dramatic angles, (say an upshot) you can inject more action and emotion into your footage.

You'll notice that this is how television documentaries and even news broadcasts work – they will switch to feeds from different cameras and even turn to face those cameras sometimes.

In other cases, different angles might come with different effects – you might switch to a portrait shot for instance that is filmed in black and white.

Don't do this on a whim though – think about what it is you're trying to communicate by adding the effect or switching the angle.

In this case you might be trying to create more 'distance', class or nostalgia.

Of course in order to switch between angles, you would normally use multiple cameras set up in different positions around the room.

This is a good strategy but it does require a bigger investment and means you'll spend more time editing and uploading your footage. A more budget approach is to use a single camera and simply change its position between takes.

The best way to get a feel for how to edit yourself in videos is to watch how others do it.

Normally, if a video has been well edited, we won't consciously notice what the camera is doing.

Watch a video you like and in a style similar to what you're going for and then pay close attention to how the angles are changing, where the speaker is being cut off and what transitions are being used (see below).

You can even try drawing up a story board and then emulating this yourself.

➤ Effects and Transitions

The editing process is also where you will begin to add things like transitions and effects.

This can also go a long way to increasing the feel of professionalism as long as you are using it well.

Try to avoid 'gimmicky' effects that distract from the content and instead only use effects like slide-ins as transitions between edits.

These should be subtle and more importantly consistent so that they're hardly noticeable.

At the very least you want to add a 'fade in' and 'fade out' effect at the beginning and end of the video, with the only exception to that rule being videos that have been purposefully designed to look amateurish.

Editing Software

To do all this you are going to need a good piece of video editing software. Windows comes with Windows Movie Maker which is a free piece of software capable of very basic editing.

While this might be enough for your needs, you'd be much better off using something a bit more premium such as Adobe Premier and After Effects.

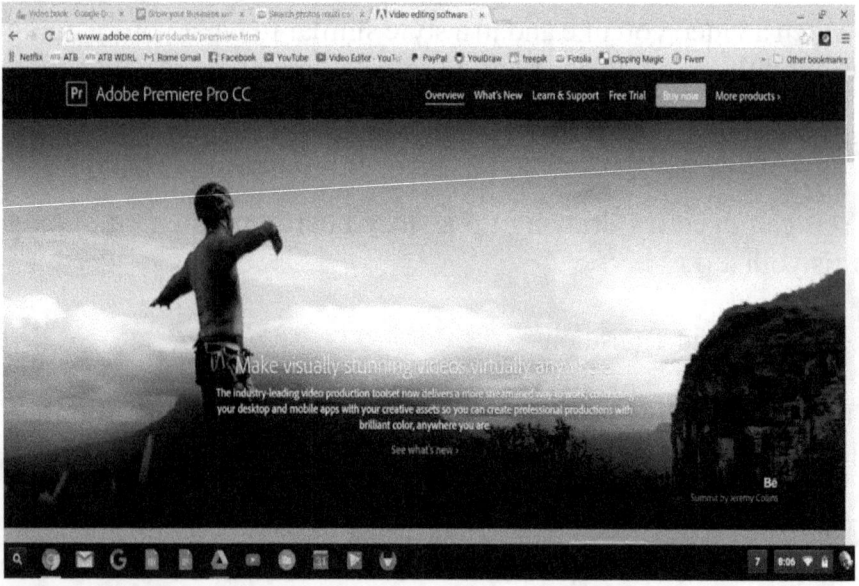

Premier is a much more feature rich piece of software that will also save you a lot of time when you're making your videos. It is a fair bit more expensive but it's worth it.

What's more, you'll get the first month free as a trial through Creative Cloud, so you can make your first few videos for free.

From there on it's a subscription based service, so you only need to pay when you actually need it for that month.

With a Creative Cloud account, you'll also get access to PhotoShop and Illustrator, both of which can be useful for creating high quality videos, so it should provide a good ROI overall.

➢ Extra Touches

Now you have a piece of well-edited footage featuring you speaking about your product/service/industry filmed on a high quality camera in a professional-looking setting, you're 70% there with your project.

You may find that your video is still missing some touches that make the most professional videos really look great. One of these is a video 'opener' or Intro.

This may not be necessary for a video that is an out-and-out commercial, but if you have a YouTube channel with tutorials, demos and other videos, then an opener can help you to build brand awareness and really add an extra level of professional quality.

Of course you can make your own opener and if you're confident with video editing software, this is a good strategy.

You don't need to do anything fancy – simply creating a montage of your own footage with a logo over the top can do the trick as can a static 'splash page' with a jingle.

A better idea is to pay someone to do it and you can do this fairly easily using a service like Fiverr.com

Fiverr is a website where hundreds of users sell a range of services all for five dollars and up. You might be surprised at the quality of work you can get here for that price.

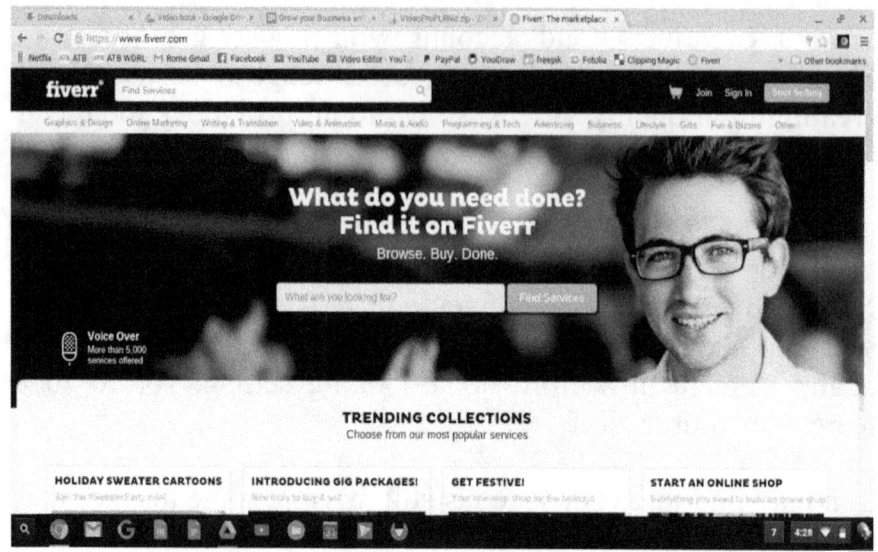

Pay someone on Fiverr to create a professional introduction for you and it will likely be far superior than anything you'd create yourself. Money well spent for the time it takes to do it well.

Likewise, you should also look into adding your logo onto the video itself.

You can do this in most good video editing software – certainly in Premier – and simply adding your logo in one of the corners can go a long way towards making the video look more professional and further enhancing your brand awareness (this also prevents anyone from stealing your footage and claiming it as their own).

If you don't already have a good logo, then this is something else you should look into arranging immediately.

Again you can get this done cheaply from various sites, including Fiverr.com or 99Designs being a good choices.

Another addition that may or may not be useful for your videos is to have screens with text.

These can be used to 'introduce' the next scene (in a video that's a list of bullet points for instance), to state questions to be answered in an interview or to share extra information such as a link to your website/pricing.

Make sure to use a unique font – you can find plenty of free ones at FontSquirrel.

Finally, and perhaps the most important 'extra touch', is your music.

Music can go a long way to increasing the professionalism of your videos and making your viewers more emotionally involved in what's happening.

Again this is something that is worth paying for, though you can get a lot of stock music from sites like stockmusic.net relatively cheaply.

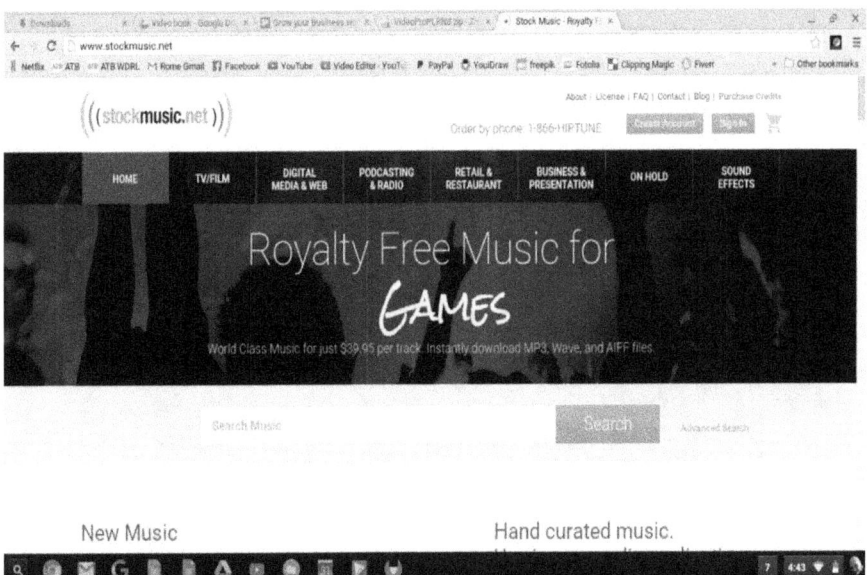

The only thing to avoid is the music provided by YouTube as that is used on so many videos that it has become generic.

If you can pay someone on Fiverr or another service to make you an original composition, then this would be preferable.

Make sure that when you add music, it doesn't drown out your voice and that you are careful to set the levels correctly.

The best backing music should fade out slightly as and when you talk and rise in volume again during times of no talking.

Make sure it fits the tone and pace of your video and try a few different tracks to find the right one.

With all these tips you'll find that it's possible to create a very professional looking and sounding video on a very low budget, and if you're very resourceful, almost free.

If you do have more money to invest, then of course another option is to hire a professional to create your videos for you or to design your video to avoid some of the challenges associated with the process.

Conclusion

In conclusion, imagine all you can do with a crazy viral video. Imagine where you could send traffic.

If 96% of consumers find videos helpful for making online purchase decisions, just imagine sending people from a video straight to a sales page, a landing page, or just your home page and even to a phone number.

As you can see, using videos effectively is vital to the ongoing success of your business. We live in an age where marketing and the Internet changes almost daily, and in order to connect with the people who will be most interested in your products and services, it is essential to make video advertising a part of that connection.

With video you can reach your current and future followers, increasing your traffic and broadening your audience. The tools you have been given here make it easy to build a winning Video Marketing campaign.

Thanks so much for the time you have taken to learn how to get the most from Video and Video Marketing. Video is here to stay in the market forever.

To Your Success.

Rome Awde

BONUS:

Go to

Book Bonus

or romeawde.com/getviralbook

for your free Cheat Sheet and Mind Map for

Video Marketing.

Resources:

Video Marketing Videos
*https://www.youtube.com/watch?v=xmgn6bEp6jQ
*https://www.youtube.com/watch?v=qghe7OuBfXw
*https://www.youtube.com/watch?v=6qkX8XqHRGE
*http://www.youtube.com/watch?v=gA_OTyzfrKA
*http://www.youtube.com/watch?v=wiOch3UBFqo
*http://www.youtube.com/watch?v=ltUTt19KkCM
*http://www.youtube.com/watch?v=vsDTKeCfcms
*http://www.youtube.com/watch?v=ACgD0uSyn8k

Video Marketing Tools
*https://www.youtube.com/watch?v=9BU7PU-jrgs
*https://www.americanexpress.com/us/small-business/openforum/
articles/10-tools-to-make-your-marketing-videos-wow/
*http://www.razorsocial.com/online-video-marketing/
*http://www.socialable.co.uk/21-of-the-best-video-marketing-tools-
for-2014/
*http://www.advisorinternetmarketing.com/tools-for-video-marketing/
*http://planetvidd.com/essential-tools-video-marketing-strategy/
*http://easyvideosuite.com/launch/
*http://localvideomarketing.biz/tool-kit/
*http://www.magnetvideo.com/content/marketing+tools/25977
*http://illuminationconsulting.com/5-great-video-creation-tools-
online-video-marketing/

Video Marketing Training
*http://www.reelmarketinginsider.com/welcome/
*http://www.slideshare.net/SoumyarW/video-making-and-marketing-
training-in-kolkata-and-howrah
*http://www.marketingsherpa.com/article/how-to/video-marketing-

tactics

*http://localvideomarketing.biz/

*http://videopower.org/free-video-marketing-course-sign-up/

*http://www.themarketingcrowd.ie/video-marketing-training.html

*http://videotrafficacademy.com/

*https://www.distilled.net/training/video-marketing-guide/

*http://www.grovo.com/create-a-youtube-video-project

Video Marketing Blogs

*http://imaginationmedia.tv/blog

*http://blog.viewbix.com/video-marketing-experts-follow-twitter/

*http://blogs.salesforce.com/company/2013/11/effective-video-marketing-throughout-the-sales-funnel.html

*http://blog.woorank.com/2014/02/online-video-marketing-important-in-2014/

*http://www.blurgroup.com/blogs/marketing/the-rise-of-video-marketing/

*http://www.smartshoot.com/blog/32-must-read-video-marketing-blog-posts/

*http://www.yume.com/blog/using-emotion-a-good-video-marketing-strategy/

*http://www.yesmediaworks.com/blog/?Preview=true/bid/19966/Video-marketing-on-YouTube

*http://www.marketingtechblog.com/video-marketing-works/

Video Marketing Forums

*http://www.warriorforum.com/warrior-special-offers/958947-method-revealed-hot-method-2014-powerful-video-marketing-blogging-hybrid-method-revealed.html

*http://www.smallbusinessbrief.com/forum/showthread.php?t=62529

*https://forum.web.com/little-business-online-video-can-grow-business/

*http://www.ukbusinessforums.co.uk/threads/video-marketing-startup-needs-beta-testers.322588/

*http://www.warriorforum.com/warrior-special-offers/927414-your-video-1st-page-google-complete-video-marketing-service-get-video-created-

Get Viral

uploaded-seod.html

Video Marketing Affiliate Marketing Programs

*https://accounts.clickbank.com/mkplSearchResult.
htm?dores=true&includeKeywords=Video%20Marketing

*http://www.offervault.com/video-affiliate-programs/?network=neverblue

*http://www.offervault.com/video-affiliate-programs/?network=maxbounty

*http://www.offervault.com/video-affiliate-programs/?network=peerfly

*http://www.offervault.com/video-affiliate-programs/?

*http://www.amazon.com/s/ref=nb_sb_noss?url=search-alias%3Daps&field-
keywords=Video+Marketing&rh=i%3Aaps%2Ck%3AVideo+Marketing

*http://www.ebay.com/sch/i.html?_odkw=Video+Marketing&gbr=1&_
fcid=1&_osacat=0&_from=R40&_clu=2&_trksid=p2045573.m570.l1313&_
nkw=Video+Marketing&_sacat=0

*https://www.jvzoo.com/products?csrf_
d=77e3a88b62799970c5adc8b11476f613&terms=Video+Marketing&cat=&subcat=

Video Marketing Demographics

*http://www.alexa.com/siteinfo/http%3A%2F%2Fwww.videobrewery.com

*http://www.alexa.com/siteinfo/www.reelseo.com

*http://www.alexa.com/siteinfo/www.tubetrackr.com

*http://www.alexa.com/siteinfo/www.revenews.com

*http://www.alexa.com/siteinfo/commandotubetools.com

*http://www.alexa.com/siteinfo/blastersuite.com

*http://www.alexa.com/siteinfo/www.youtube.com

*http://www.alexa.com/siteinfo/dailymotion.com

*http://www.alexa.com/siteinfo/metacafe.com

*http://www.alexa.com/siteinfo/vimeo.com

*http://www.alexa.com/siteinfo/vube.com

Video Marketing Webinars

*http://www.youtube.com/watch?v=5-Ryu9VnnQY

*http://www.youtube.com/watch?v=-x-EpeXSbzc

*http://www.youtube.com/watch?v=C_49hMFkye8&list=PLK9OhVcw_
LCqqBqQIFut1Jn4foWEsVxYv

*http://www.youtube.com/watch?v=DcZ0JUo8RwM

*http://www.youtube.com/watch?v=tNMzmXhKB74&list=PLCb_
hQEZ7Z14lRpouUdN5XVCd-jPK0s2v
*http://blog.vidcaster.com/5-video-marketing-webinars/
*http://www.youtube.com/watch?v=JAyfjBoKOYk
*http://www.youtube.com/watch?v=DgcJf7aUfO4
*http://www.youtube.com/watch?v=9V23AYgjlp0
*http://www.youtube.com/watch?v=tNMzmXhKB74

Video Marketing Infographics
*http://infographicb2b.com/category/video-marketing-infographics/
*http://www.istockphoto.com/article_view.php?ID=1590#.U8RW_mgtFDo
*http://contently.com/strategist/2013/03/20/the-ultimate-case-for-
video-marketing-infographic/
*http://www.business2community.com/infographics/the-importance-of-
video-marketing-infographic-0529729
*http://www.prestigemarketing.ca/blog/your-video-marketing-handbook-
infographic/
*http://www.socialmediatoday.com/content/video-marketing-social-
proof-numbers-infographic
*http://blog.newscred.com/article/top-10-content-marketing-infographi
cs/1ae4735cbce964d146a98e948559384a

Video Marketing Facts
*http://blog.viewbix.com/tweetable-video-marketing-facts/
*http://www.business2community.com/content-marketing/16-facts-video-
marketing-will-keep-night-0844491
*http://www.youtube.com/watch?v=B3IuJrEVaoo
*https://smallbusiness.yahoo.com/advisor/23-tweetable-video-
marketing-facts-know-053943274.html
*http://visual.ly/video-marketing-facts
*http://www.ddshosting.com/fast-facts-need-know-video-marketing/

NOTES:

www.ingramcontent.com/pod-product-compliance
Lightning Source LLC
Chambersburg PA
CBHW060349190526
45169CB00002B/532